Then Came A Miracle

Then Came A Miracle

Jama Kehoe Bigger

Fleming H. Revell Company
Old Tappan, New Jersey

Scripture quotations in this volume are from the King
James Version of the Bible.

Library of Congress Cataloging in Publication Data

Bigger, Jama Kehoe.
    Then came a miracle.

      1. Bigger, Jama Kehoe. 2. Christian biography—
United States. 3. Miracles. I. Title.
BR1725.B49A34   280'.4'0924 [B]   81–12063
ISBN 0–8007–1275–7   AACR2

To
Mom and Dad,
Steve, Doug, and Julee—
whose love and faith and
strength made this book
possible . . .

Contents

Acknowledgements

My deepest gratitude to my family and my friends, especially those I have lived with, for their support and encouragement over the several years that I was writing this book. And special thanks to Tom Mullen, Floyd Thatcher, and my friends at the Midwest Writer's Workshop. Fritz Ridenour also did a sensitive job of editing my rough draft, which I appreciate; he even allowed me to keep a few semicolons. I thank Victor Oliver, too, for his faith in my writing ability. Most importantly, a big hug and kiss to my husband, John, for his patience and understanding during the first six months of our marriage when I was working on the final drafts of my manuscript. To those who gave to me, it shall be returned to them, multiplied.

Jama Kehoe Bigger

Introduction

The door slammed shut. I was safe and protected in an ark, made not of gopher wood like Noah's, but of faith. It was an ark of grace, mercy, and compassion, built by the Lord to house one mother who needed it. Jama, our second child and first daughter, was paralyzed from the neck down after a diving accident.

During the first days after the accident, I thought that I was totally in His rest concerning Jama, but God always knows the depths and hidden parts of our hearts. He knew my agony and frustration when she cried out to me to hold her, kiss her, and tell Jesus to make the hurt go away. But I couldn't pick her up and cradle her in my arms with the tongs in her skull and the bottles draining into her veins. My kiss would not make the hurt go away as she lay strapped to a Stryker Frame.

Only Jesus was the answer. He knew that I needed an intensity of faith and an abiding trust that I had never experienced before. And so it was there, in my ark of faith, that God established His covenant with me. Psalms 50:15 said I could call upon Him in my time of trouble and He would deliver me. And I would give Him the glory for all that He would do in my daughter's life.

Since the day I entered my ark, I never doubted God's Word. When God's Word is planted and deeply rooted in your heart, the waters may rise, but they will never wash away His truth. Many times things were said to make me see "the reality of Jama's situation." But God implanted upon my heart a greater reality: His Word is true, and healing is in His Word. That Word was for Jama. As Noah's ark was a place of safety in the storms, so was my ark a haven of total trust for me. Once you have surrendered to God, He will keep you. I could not offer a sacrifice to God as Noah did; instead, I let praise be continually in my mouth as my sacrifice to Him. It was—and is—wonderful!

Jama is a girl that you will identify with. You will laugh with her, cry with her, but most of all you will be inspired by her faith in the Living God.

We were a very normal, active family who had a tragedy befall them. We are not the first family to have this happen, nor will we be the last. What we did with this tragedy is the basis for this book. It is a book about a courageous young girl with a faith in God that would not be denied. Her story is one of victory. Victory because of her love of Jesus and her expectancy that He would see her through every circumstance and challenge that came her way. You will marvel at her maturity in Christ as a child, and then you'll rejoice to see her growth as she moves through the teen years and on to college.

Over eleven years have passed since Jama dove into that swimming pool on a hot, July day. God is still moving in all our lives to shape them for His glory. Again and again we have asked Him to help us to love mercy and walk humbly with our God. That is what this book is all about—Jama's walk with God.

May the Father enrich your life and draw you close to Him as you share Jama's pain—and triumph.

Barbara Kehoe

Who fed thee in the wilderness with manna, which thy fathers knew not, that he might humble thee, and that he might prove thee, to do thee good at thy latter end.

Deuteronomy 8:16

Then Came A Miracle

1
The Dive

The chlorine burned fear into my eyes as I watched my arms floating in the water. I looked down at my legs; they wouldn't move, either. My squatting body was immersed in four feet of water, but I couldn't get my head up for air.

My God! My God! Dear Jesus! Help me get up! Don't let me drown! Please! Please, God! Don't let me die! I prayed. I pleaded. I felt the pressure in my lungs; my chest was tightening in a vise of water. The chlorine burned deeper as my eyes searched the water for someone to help me. Cries and pleas, rebellion against death, craving for air violently flamed inside my skull, my lungs, my soul. *Please, God! I'm only thirteen! Air! I need air!*

A trim young girl in a green tanksuit, her blond hair buoyant in the waves and splashings, swam closer. *Christy! Dear God, it's Christy!* I had to get her attention. I had to let her know that I was hurt. I screamed with a force I had never used before, "Help!" The sound echoed under the water and returned to me; bubbles bounced to the surface; water rushed down my throat. Christy nodded, grinning broadly, and blurted out a yell in mimicry. Panic peaked. *O God, God,* my heart whispered with more resignation than force. *I gave You my life. Don't let me die. Let me serve You.*

Christy nudged my floating arm. I saw her do it, but felt nothing; it was as if it were not a part of my body. I tightened my eyes in agony as I saw her spring above the water. A rolling fog was beginning to creep over my consciousness.

Then gulps of air surged into my lungs. Water sputtered from my mouth; I coughed and gasped. Christy was grasping my shoulders; my wet hair hung in my face.

17

"Christy!" I heard my hoarse voice. "Help me or I'll drown. Something's wrong. I can't move." Fear flamed in my eyes. I saw her tanned face turn white and heard a short, nervous laugh.

"You're kidding, aren't you, Jama?" Her blue eyes pleaded for a yes.

"No, Christy, I'm not. I'm hurt. I can't move my legs. Help me." I blinked away streams of chlorine water that dripped from my hair.

"Patty!" Christy shouted. A girl from across the pool came swimming over. "Jama's hurt. Hold her shoulders here while I go get the lifeguard." Patty obeyed; her eyes were full of questions, but she asked none. I couldn't think. I only breathed.

Before Christy could come back with the lifeguard, a lady grabbed me under the arms and pulled me out of the pool. My body scraped against the concrete surface; I felt nothing. I saw my arms and legs fall in a heap on the deck. When I was just out of the water, the lifeguard came and picked me up as he would a baby, even though he had a cast on his wrist. He carried me into the office, where the manager and another guard hustled to put towels on the floor so he could lay me out straight. The manager's face was ashen when he bent down and questioned me. His eyes were dark, and under his dark hair, just touched with gray, his forehead was wrinkled with concern.

"Where does it hurt?"

"I don't know. I can't feel anything. I'm numb all over. I don't hurt, but I can't move. I don't know what happened. I was just diving." The calmness of my voice surprised me. I told him my telephone number so he could call my parents.

It's hard for me to remember the sequence of events after that. I remember wanting to see Christy, wanting to tell her that I didn't hurt. She had followed the lifeguard to the screen door of the office, and over his shoulder, I had seen her face shadowed with worry. I wondered what she was thinking. Later, when she came to visit me in the hospital, she said that she couldn't think; she had gone to the snack bar and had a frosted malt, silently.

It seemed that in no time at all, I heard Dad's voice coming by the front desk and back into the office. From my cocoon of towels, only my head showing, I raised my eyes backward as far as my stationary position would allow and saw Dad's upside-down smile.

"Hi, honey."

"Hi, Dad."

The manager, the lifeguard, and Dad slowly moved me from the office to the back of our station wagon, where Dad had put the seat down. They held me steady, supporting my head, my middle, and my feet. As Dad shut the door, I saw the manager pull him aside. The man still had that worried look on his face. Dad patted his shoulder. I wanted to tell him before we left that I would be okay, but he walked slowly back to the screen door.

When we were on the way home, I realized that I couldn't feel the bumps and jolts of the moving car. I couldn't piece together the events that had occurred and the reasons why I was the way I was—unmoving and unfeeling.

"So, tell me what happened, Jama. No one could tell me anything over the phone, only that you were hurt."

"I don't know, Dad. Like I've been telling everyone, all we were doing were dives. We were trying to see who could make the goofiest face before going into the water. I made a pretty good racing dive, got up, ran a little ways down the deck, and dove again. I don't remember hitting the bottom of the pool. I didn't feel anything but the cold water as I was diving in. Then, when I opened my eyes, I couldn't get up out of the water. I thought I was going to drown. I was praying hard, Dad. Then Christy came and lifted my shoulders up."

"Well we're almost home. We'll get you inside and pray immediately. Mom's waiting."

I wanted to be home. The thought of rushing me to the hospital never occurred to me, nor did it to Dad. Going home for prayer was all I wanted. I knew God would heal me no matter what was wrong.

While Dad was driving home, Mom was becoming more concerned. She excused herself from the living room where she had been talking with our guests, Mel and Ginny. Sitting silently at the kitchen table, she pulled a Scripture card from our Daily Bread box. She needed some word of comfort.

"And call upon me in the day of trouble: I will deliver thee, and thou shalt glorify me" (Psalms 50:15). She whispered the words slowly and knew that something serious had happened. Laying her head down on the table, her arms for a cushion, she prayed for comfort and for strength against what was unknown.

At the sound of the station wagon pulling into the driveway, she was out the front door. As her short legs carried her from the porch, down the three steps—taken as one—and to the car, a voice inside her persisted: *Broken neck, broken neck.* With all her faith, she declared, *No! We will have no broken necks in this house.*

When I heard the car door open, I remember wanting so desperately to see Mom, but I couldn't raise my head to look down at my feet, where she was standing. I heard her whisper, "Jama . . . Jama."

"Let's get you inside, honey. Barb, why don't you go clear everything off Steve's bed. We'll carry her in there, since it's downstairs," Dad instructed.

Holding the towels at the corners, Dad and Mel carefully moved me into the house. But as we were going up the porch steps, my body at a sagging angle, my leg fell out of the towel and hit the cement step. I saw it slipping; the message went to the brain: *Pull your leg back onto the towel, Jama.* I saw it hit and waited for the pain to dart from my ankle through my leg. I didn't feel anything.

"Dad, my leg, my leg," my panic repeated. They stopped.

"It's okay, Jama. I'll get it." Dad reached down and gently lifted my leg back onto the towel. A heavy boulder of fear crashed and splintered thoughts into the tenderness of my brain. I couldn't feel the cement; I couldn't move my legs. *Dear Jesus! What's wrong with me? Let me move!*

The memories of that night ebb from remembering the tiny grains of sand on the shore, to becoming lost in a sea of vagueness. I remember the beginnings of pain that ricocheted from the back of my neck to the base of my skull when Mom inched the swimming suit from my body and slipped a nightgown over my head as I lay flat on the bed. And I remember the warm hands of Mom and Dad on my head as they prayed fervently for God's touch on my body. I tried to pray away the fear when I saw them move their hands to my arms and I couldn't feel them.

Then my older brother Steve came in to see how I was, and I apologized for taking his bed from him. He grinned, "It's okay." The light reflected off his blond hair.

And shy Doug, who was then twelve, peeked his head in the doorway. I barely heard his question, "Are you going to be all right, Jama?"

"I think so," I told him.

Finally, Julee, a timid eight-year-old when anything turned serious, tiptoed in and just stood by the bed, saying nothing for a long time, her little eyes telling her love. But before she left, she whispered, "I'm praying real hard for you." I wanted to hug her.

My awareness of the weekly youth meeting we had at our house that evening was fogged in pain. The meeting was held in the living room; and if I concentrated, I could hear much of the singing and sharing from my bed in Steve's room. However, all my concentration was focused on muffling the desire to cry and scream the pain away. In one room there was joy and singing and clapping hands; in the other room, there was pain and crying and a motionless body.

But one moment pierced the fog in my mind like a lighthouse beam. Before the kids left, Dad told them about my accident, since they wanted to know why I hadn't joined them. Then Dad asked them to pray for me. They squeezed into Steve's room, clasped hands, some knelt beside the bed, and with tender hearts and expectant faith, they lifted me up to God in their prayers. Dual tears of pain and comfort silently slid from my eyes. I felt reassured that whatever was wrong would be taken care of.

As the prayers flowed into a peace of silent thanksgiving, my heart admonished my mind. Yes, after all, God would take care of me. Hadn't I given Him my life two years ago, and hadn't He always been faithful to answer all my prayers since then? Would He deny me now? No, my faith told me. I had memorized much

Scripture in those two years, and I knew that if I asked, it would be given to me; and if I sought, I would find. The icy tentacles of fear started to melt under the heat of His presence.

After everyone finally left, Mom and Dad set up a cot and put a sleeping bag on the floor so they could stay with me throughout the night. They wanted to be near me, to pray for me. Because of my mom's renewed relationship with the Lord, our whole family had decided that the best way to live was to walk as closely to Jesus as possible. In these two years, we had been learning to depend upon God as our source for every need. Praying soon became our first thought and action concerning any problem. In faith we began trusting God to supply our family's smallest needs. We didn't even have a bottle of aspirin in the house.

Now as Mom and Dad sat on the bed beside me, holding my hand and touching my face, we prayed in our strongest faith for my healing. We claimed the Bible's promises for healing, remembering when God declared, "I am the Lord that healeth thee" (Exodus 15:26). We knew that God could heal, and heal immediately, as we had all seen the quick recoveries from sprained ankles, broken thumbs, and severe headaches.

"We've prayed and believed, and now it's done. All we have to do now is stand, right?" Dad said as we opened our eyes from praying.

"Right," Mom and I agreed in unison.

They both kissed me good-night and Dad turned out the light. In the darkness the pain seemed magnified, and I longed for the escape of sleep. The tears fell from my eyes; I fought to control the sobs. Mom, in her quiet, soothing voice, reached across from the cot and prayed, "Touch her, Father. Touch her."

Every now and then I dozed, but then bolts of pain jerked me from sleep. To quiet my sobbing, Mom came and held me—mother and child—but she couldn't hold back the pain.

As I fought to divorce the pain from sleep, God ministered to each of us. He spoke with comforting promises. In a dream, Dad saw me walking again, but my steps were short and halting like those of a small child, as if I were learning to walk all over again. Mom saw my back, all scraped and bleeding, and she wondered whether I had scraped it somehow on the bottom of the pool. But as she looked, the cuts moved to become the stripes on Jesus' back, forming the word *Jesus*. She woke up remembering the Scripture ". . . by [His] stripes ye were healed" (1 Peter 2:24).

Their words, carrying hope and balm, floated through the night air that was filled with the sound of my sobs. I held them to my heart. The night seemed interminable. I lost all connection with time, and the darkness and pain became one. Lying on my back, I drifted into sleep. I saw myself turned on my stomach, my favorite sleeping position, but I was crying because of the pain. Then, in between the tears, I saw two feet come before me. I knew it was Jesus. He came and stood by my bed; all I could see were His sandaled feet and the hem of His robe. I couldn't see His face because I couldn't turn over. Lightly, His warm touch was on my back. The pain was gone. I slept until daylight.

I awoke with a start; another bolt of pain tore through my head. My cheeks were moist, and I knew that I had been crying in my sleep. Mom and Dad had gone out of the room, and I could hear their voices in the kitchen. I couldn't hear what they were saying, and soon their voices faded as I stared at the morning light streaking a banner across the wall, the light reflecting off Steve's golf trophies. I stared and thought and prayed, *Please, God, take this pain away. I believe that You've healed me. Please let me feel it.*

Mom and Dad came back into the room and sat beside me once again. Mom brushed away a tear that had started the familiar path from my eye to my ear.

"Honey, we've been talking about taking you to the hospital. What do you think about that?" Dad asked.

"Dad, the pain is really bad, and my head and neck seem to hurt more and more. Maybe we should go."

"Well, your mother and I are also concerned because you haven't gone to the bathroom since we brought you home, and you drank a lot of 7-Up last night. We just called Dr. McDowell next door, and he said that we should call an ambulance. Now, don't think that by going to the hospital you don't have faith. God works through doctors, too." He kissed my forehead and went to call for an ambulance. Mom stayed and wiped away my tears and stroked my hair, which was long and stringy from not being combed after it had dried.

I left the sad faces of my brothers and sister and our guests at 9:30 A.M. on July 25, 1969, and went to the emergency room at Ball Memorial Hospital in Muncie, Indiana. I had no idea how long it would be before I was once again in our house with my family.

Dad had also called our family doctor, Dr. Warren Bergwall, about the accident. When the ambulance pulled in, he was there waiting. A neurosurgeon, Dr. Charles Goodell, also met us. I've forgotten the details of the examination and x-raying because of the exhaustion I felt and the passing of time. However, I do remember the sight and sounds of one room in which the nurses stopped my cart. Mom and Dad waited outside each room for me, and I saw love in their eyes as each door was closed.

My eyes squeezed shut on reflex as I was moved beneath rows of glaring, piercing lights, but the lights were too bright and penetrated my eyelids.

"What are you going to do to me?" I asked the nurse.

"I just gave you a local anesthetic to make you sleep. Relax." Her words were soft, and I felt myself give way to sleep. The pain in my head and neck had waned since I had received a shot for pain earlier. Now, all I wanted to do was sleep. A loud sound suddenly vibrated me back to consciousness. A loud buzzing sound.

"What are you doing to me?" I mumbled.

Dr. Goodell answered, "I'm afraid I have to shave your hair off so we can put you in traction. Just relax; you won't feel a thing." But I did feel something: his hand pulling my hair back and the cold clippers running from my forehead all the way down my scalp. Tears of exhaustion and teenage vanity poured forth.

"Please, please, don't cut my hair!" I sobbed. "Couldn't you just cut it where the traction goes? You don't understand. I've been letting it grow. Please don't cut my long hair!" The words came babbling through my sobs; the tears waterlogged my ears.

"I'm sorry, Jama. But I have to cut it. It'll grow back. Now close your eyes. Relax. Go to sleep. It'll be over in a little while."

Easy for you to say, I thought. *It'll grow back, ha!* I wanted to cry at him, "Do you know how long I've been trying to let my hair grow?" In my mind I could see all my hair falling in sun-streaked clumps to the floor. Amid the cacophony of buzzing and sobs, I finally fell through the barrier that divided the conscious from the unconscious. I couldn't fight the power of the drug anymore. *My hair, my hair,* I remember thinking.

In a tunnel darkened on all sides, a small light glowed in the distance. My body floated toward it, as if drifting downstream, pulled by a magnetic force. The pulling increased, and I wanted to stop the motion, to go back—back into the waters of forgetfulness that had no memory of the pulling. The light became brighter. I tried to squeeze my eyes together to force the light and the pain away. I kept my eyes closed, even though I knew I had been pulled out of the tunnel and across those waters of forgetfulness into consciousness.

Long fingers of pain stretched from my neck and surrounded the top of my head. The pain pulled my head so far backward that my chin was perpendicular to the ceiling. I opened my eyes. The only movement that I could make was the slow rotation of my eyes, scanning above and to the sides. My peripheral vision told me that I had been moved to another room. *Oh, my hair!* I remembered. My hands wanted to reach for my head to feel for my hair. Desperately, I hoped that I'd dreamt the conversation with Dr. Goodell. Perhaps he didn't really tell me that he was shaving my head. But I couldn't move to find out the truth, and that only added to my frustration and despair. I knew the crying would start and my ears would fill up again if I didn't get control of myself.

I looked around the room again with what limited vision I had. I remember trying to figure out why a long bar about eighteen inches above me was connecting the head and the foot of the bed. I tried to take a quick glance at my feet, but the grip of pain tightened on my head and the back of my neck. It seized me with an iron force and the grasp shortened my breathing. I closed my eyes again. Quiet sobs caught in my throat as I tried to pray for relief, but the pain cut short any long conversations with God.

"Jesus, Jesus," I sobbed, blinking the tears from my eyes. Self-pity rolled in. *What am I to do? Why do I hurt so bad?* Then came a wave of loneliness. I wanted my mom and daddy. The tears poured forth as the pain raged in my heart and head.

"Nurse?" The curtain that hung around my bed was rolled back on its ball bearings by a nurse, revealing the nurses' station. "Please, will you do something for my pain? I can't stand it." I didn't want to be crying so uncontrollably, and I felt ashamed. But I couldn't help it, and the more I tried not to, the more I cried. The nurse pulled a tissue from a box on the bedstand and wiped my wet face.

"Okay. Just a minute. I'll be right back. Try not to cry. It will only pull on your head more."

I closed my eyes and waited for the squish, squish sound of her returning steps. "Where are my mom and dad?" I asked when she had returned.

"They went home for a while to get some rest. They'll be back shortly." Her tone was professional, but comforting. Straining my eyes downward as much as possible to see what she was doing, I saw her raise the empty needle. I hadn't felt the injection. I sighed and closed my eyes again, trying to concentrate on God, trying not to question Him, waiting for my parents to come to me, waiting for the painkiller to melt away the agony. In two days—just thirty-six hours—my life had been changed from a carefree adolescence to a constant struggle with pain.

2

ICU

Time and pain became allied. I was conscious of time only when conscious of pain. Every few hours I awakened, crying, and a nurse injected me with another shot for pain. The cloak of pain wrapped tightly around my head and neck; reality was blanketed by sleep and strange drug-induced dreams.

Hospital regulations allowed my parents to visit me in the Intensive Care Unit every four hours around the clock. They never missed a visit, sometimes coming together, sometimes alone; and though my mind was hazed by the drugs, I always knew when they were there. Visitors were permitted ten to fifteen minutes, and those minutes were priceless to me. The pain seemed less when Mom and Dad were there, and when they had to leave, I cried like a four-year-old left with a babysitter. Whatever grown-up fortitude I thought I possessed was dwarfed by my childlike needs to be with those I loved and who loved me: with my mother, who had always rocked me and whispered the Twenty-third Psalm in my ear whenever I was sick or hurting; with my father, who had carried me upstairs to my bedroom when I was sick or had fallen asleep on the couch; with my brothers and sister, who spoke their love and concern by bringing Kleenexes and changing TV channels.

During those moments when I was alone, the traction seemed to pull a greater pain through my head. The tears spilled from the corners of my eyes and trailed into my ears. And I waited for Mom or Dad to come with a deep aching.

"Oh, Mom," I sobbed when I saw her small form pulling back the curtain that isolated me from the other patients.

"I'm right here, honey." She kissed my cheek and stroked my forehead where my bangs had been.

"Mom, my ears are full of tears. Oh, I'm so glad you're here. I hurt so bad. I wish you could hold me, and rock me, and ask Jesus to take the pain away. Oh, Mom," I sobbed again, spilling more tears.

"I know, honey. I wish I could hold you too." Her lips tightened and she leaned over me, stretching on tiptoe, and laying across me very lightly. "That's not a very good hug, but in my heart I'm holding you. And Jesus is holding you; He'll take the pain away."

"Thanks, Mom. I know He will. Mom, will you help me blow my nose?"

"Sure." With a tissue she wiped the tears out of my ears, then held it over my nose. "Blow."

I obeyed, feeling like a child again.

Mom stayed by the bed, talking quietly to me about the friends who had called, and soon the nurse politely informed us that ten minutes had passed.

"Dad will be in at midnight. He's with your Aunt Billie and Uncle Harley right now. And then I'll be in at four. You get some rest now, okay? I love you." She bent down to kiss me again and I started to cry. "Don't cry, Jama, please. You'll get tears in your ears again." Her voice pleaded tenderly, slightly cracking.

"I'm trying not to. I love you, Mom. Tell Steve and Doug and Julee that I love them and miss them."

"I will. I love you, Jama." She reached for the curtain. "And so does Jesus," she added. "I'll see you soon." She left and I felt an emptiness.

Mom hadn't cried when she was with me, but my tears of pain affected the mother in her. As soon as she got home and saw my dad, she fell into his arms, crying, "Oh, Fred, I can't help her! She wanted me to hold her tonight, to ask Jesus to take the pain away. She wanted me to do all the things I used to do to console her. But her pain is beyond a kiss and a hug, and I can't help her." She sobbed into Dad's shoulder; he held her tightly.

"I know, honey. I know." His voice was soft; he knew her heart. "Harley and Billie are in the dining room. Let's go in and we'll pray."

Slowly they walked arm in arm into the dining room. Mom hugged her younger brother and sister-in-law, hugs of concern and sorrow; she knew that they, too, were praying for me. After sitting around the table, they all held hands, forming a circle of love. Dad's firm voice began to pray; his spirit prayed, and his words mounted in assurance and volume. As he prayed, a calmness came to Mom, and she knew that God understood a mother's pain. The tears that flowed as Dad finished praying were tears of sweet comfort and not bitter despair.

Doug and Julee were too young and were not allowed to visit me in Intensive Care, but they wrote notes and drew pictures and sent them via Mom and Dad. Doug, who rarely displayed his love in any way other than teasing, wrote me a note telling me how much he missed me and that he was praying for my hair to grow back and for me to get well. He signed it, "Doug your brother who loves you. PTLA." I cried when Mom read the tender message. *Yes, Doug,* I thought, *I'll praise the Lord always.*

Because he was fourteen, Steve was allowed to come. He was the loving elder brother. Our one-year difference seemed more, as his face and eyes mirrored his maturity. He told me about our friends who had called to ask how I was. As he read each card to me, he held it at an angle so I could see. He read to me from the Bible or from Charles Sheldon's *In His Steps,* which Mom had brought from home. I never wanted him to see my pain; but he knew, and sometimes he would just stand quietly beside the bed and hold my hand.

Between visits I slept. I wanted to escape the pain and the loneliness. The drugs not only deadened the pain so I could sleep, they also numbed my senses, fuddling ideas and muffling sounds as I came in and out of a thick cloud of drugged sleep. Most of the memories of that time have been shadowed by that thick cloud; however, one incident I remember well. I was surfacing to consciousness when I thought I heard a nurse's voice, soft, yet clear, saying, "I see you." My mind still in a mist, I thought, *What a funny thing to say. Of course she sees me, I'm right next to her desk. Is she trying to play a game with me?*

"Nurse?" I whispered, rolling my eyes to the far right and noticing the open curtain. She was sitting at the nurses' desk, looking directly at me, smiling, the telephone to her ear. She raised her finger up to indicate, Just a minute. When she hung up and came to my bed, I asked, "Why did you just say, 'I see you?' I know you see me. I'm right here." Then I teased, "Were you trying to play peek-a-boo?"

She started to laugh and I thought, *Oh, boy, I've said something real dumb again.* Her "no" came out in a long giggle, "Not *I* see *you,*" she said, pointing to herself and then to me, "but ICU, the abbreviation for Intensive Care Unit. I always say that when I answer the phone. It saves time."

Then I started to laugh. Boy, talk about dumb! What a mistake: ICU—*I see you!* No wonder she was laughing. Laughter rumbled inside, abandoned emotions amplified by the drugs, shaking my body, jerking my head, jolting my traction. Tears of laughter mingled with tears of pain. I didn't care. I still laughed, and the nurse laughed. She put her finger to her mouth, shushing us both, because of the sleeping patients, but I couldn't stop. I had made a polaric leap from sorrow to mirth; the tears became a therapeutic release.

"I feel *so* dumb! I didn't even hear the phone ring!" I laughed with embarrassment. "Oh, my head!" My skull ached, but still I laughed.

Settling down took a few minutes. Just as I would stop laughing, I would roll my eyes back in unbelief at how dumb I had been, and the giggles would start again. When Mom and Dad came a little while later, I had to tell them the story, which only started the painful laughter again; we all laughed together. The comic relief lasted for days—and I needed relief.

When I had entered the hospital, Dr. Goodell had prescribed a traction treatment of twenty-five pounds to pull my spinal cord back into alignment. My spinal cord had been crushed but not severed at the moment of injury, and pieces of the vertebral bone were pressing into it, causing a curvature and the paralysis. My head had been shaved, and two small holes were drilled into my skull to anchor the traction. The traction looked like an ice tong; in fact, it was called Crutchfield tongs. The weight of the traction was suspended from these tongs. The long bar, which ran above me the length of the bed, was connected to a frame, a Stryker Frame. This Stryker was flipped every two hours—stomach to back, back to stomach—to equalize the traction.

By Sunday, two days after I had been admitted, the pain was so excruciating that I became a slave to the painkilling injections. That night my parents told me that Dr. Goodell had said I needed an operation, a laminectomy, during which he would remove vertebral posterior arches, which were the pieces that were causing the pressure on my spinal cord.

Learning what was wrong with me was like taking a short course in anatomy. The spinal cord runs down the body through the center of the vertebral column, which begins with seven cervical vertebrae. Each vertebra consists of a vertebral body on the back of which is fixed an arch. These vertebrae resemble rings through which the spinal cord passes.

Whether the accident occurred because of the angle and the force with which I entered the pool, or whether I struck the bottom of the pool with my head, I don't know because I had no bumps or abrasions, and I never lost consciousness. But the severe impact caused the body of the fifth cervical vertebra to be pulled and shattered into the spinal cord. The initial X rays indicated that I had a compressed fracture of the body of the fifth cervical vertebra and an incomplete dislocation at the fifth and sixth cervical level. Normally, the vertebral bodies are in a line, but my injury had caused the body of the fifth cervical vertebra, or C5, to be ruptured and unaligned with the bodies of the fourth and sixth vertebrae. Dislocation with or without fracture causes profound disability because of the immobility of the cervical region. In layman's terms, I had a broken neck.

I didn't learn until much later how severe my injury had been, that the higher the cord damage, the poorer the prognosis. The hospital staff was first of all concerned with keeping me alive. I didn't know that the neural tissue of the spinal cord is very delicate and if destroyed does not regenerate or regain function. In about 95 percent of all cord injuries, the damage is done at the instant of the injury, and there is never any recovery. The patient is paralyzed for life.

Nor would I learn until later the term *quadriplegic*—a term that refers to one who is paralyzed in all four extremities. The patient has not only motor or movement damage, but sensory damage as well, so that he can't move or feel anything below the area of injury. Often he will recover some gross muscle movement, but not fine, sensitive motor control.

Dr. Goodell's neurological examination revealed the extent of my damage: I was sensitive to touch below the knee on the right side and on the outside portion of my left leg. My legs, however, had no muscle tone, no normal tension or responsiveness. The only motion response was feeble flexing movement, a slight twitch when the sole of my foot was stimulated by a pin prick. This could have been due to an involuntary nerve reflex response, because I could not feel the prick to send a message of pain to my brain and then withdraw my foot. I was also insensitive to pain over the upper part of the lower legs and over my thighs.

The report on the upper part of my body was equally discouraging. The muscles that extend my arms and forearms, the triceps, were completely paralyzed. So were the flexor forearm muscles and the intrinsic hand muscles. My hands were clenched fists that would not open. However, I did have good strength in the deltoid muscles of the shoulder, which flex my arms and forearms, and in the biceps muscles which turn my hands so that the palms face upward. Very slowly, I could rotate my arms to turn my fists toward the ceiling and slightly bend my arms at the elbows.

The prognosis for a patient with this kind of neurological damage to the fifth cervical vertebra is that he cannot roll over or come to a sitting position in bed, he has no use of his hands, and he cannot walk. He is confined to a wheelchair. But I didn't know any of this. I just knew that for some reason I couldn't move or feel anything.

As the surgery time on Monday evening steadily approached, so did anxiety. Fear fluttered freely in my stomach. I had never had an operation before. *What if I never wake up?* I thought. *Well, I'll be with Jesus,* I consoled myself. But still, I couldn't sleep, so I prayed and tried mentally to sing as many songs as I could remember to keep from thinking about what was going to happen.

And when I was flipped on my stomach, I read Dad's big, black Bible which he had put on the board beneath the Stryker Frame. Not being able to reach down to turn the pages, I read and reread Psalm 91. I whispered the words to myself, feeling their power, their promise. God's presence prevailed over fear. "For he shall give his angels charge over me, to keep me in all my ways" (*see* v. 11).

After the anesthesiologist injected me with his medicine, I was carted, face down, into the hallway to be taken to the operating room. A nurse removed the board beneath me, and I stared at the patterned tiles on the floor. Hearing footsteps, I saw a pair of man's shoes walking up and a pair of lady's shoes clicking behind them.

"Is that you, Mom and Dad?" I asked, wanting to see not their shoes, but their faces. Above the feet, I heard their voices.

"We're right here, Jama." Dad's voice was tender. I felt pressure on my shoulder and knew they had their hands on me for comfort and reassurance. He bent down, and his words were gentle in my ears. "I love you, sweetheart. Jesus is with you; you'll be all right."

"I love you, too, honey," Mom whispered in my other ear. "You have people all over the city and all our relatives praying for you." I wanted to be rocked and to cry into her shoulder, but instead the tears splattered noiselessly onto the floor. The anesthetic billowed over my senses. Closing my eyes, I sobbed softly, "Oh, Mom. Dad." I heard Mom sigh and felt the motion of the cart as a nurse pushed me toward the operating room. *Jesus, Jesus,* I repeated in my mind as the anesthetic pushed me over the brink into unconsciousness.

After the operation, the blackness was heavy and deep. I pushed and pushed against it, only to have it crash down on me again as soon as I would relax my effort. The darkness rolled back just long enough for my eyes to peek open, then drove me back into a deep, dreamless sleep once more. I rocked back and forth on waves of consciousness and unconsciousness; sounds floated in and out as if someone were playing with a volume control. The drugged sleep shrouded impressions that make memories.

Under the doctor's orders, I was turned every two hours, and gradually I became aware of the process again. Surfing up on a wave of consciousness, I watched as a nurse placed a lambskin over my chest and legs; another nurse laid a two-inch board over the lambskin, strapping everything together. With one nurse at the foot of the bed and the other at the head, they flipped me 180 degrees, simultaneously, quickly, and carefully, always mindful of the traction since the smallest jar would shoot bullets of pain through my head.

As I watched, I tried to swallow; my mouth was dust dry. I couldn't lick my lips. "Nurse," I croaked, "could I please have some water?"

"No, I'm sorry," she answered. "The doctor said you weren't to have anything."

"But all I want is a drink of water. You don't have to get me anything to eat." I pleaded in desperation.

"He has 'ice chips' written on your chart."

"Yes, please. Could I have some?"

I let the small ice chip she placed on my lips melt over their parchedness a little before letting my tongue lick the rest of it into nothing. I sucked that coldness down my throat, one ice chip after another, until she had fed me the entire cup. And still I wanted more. The dry throat and the parched lips were soothed, but the desire for a long, cold drink lingered, ice-cold water that I could swish around in my mouth and swallow in large gulps.

Then hunger became the companion to thirst, stalking in my mind with a tray of temptations: thick hamburgers with melted cheese, pepperoni pizza covered with mozzarella, chocolate chip cookies warm from the oven, icy Dr. Peppers. For two days after the operation, I was prohibited from eating or drinking anything; and for two days I begged the nurses to sneak me something, anything—crumbs, scraps. I told them that the lambskin on the Stryker was beginning to look like lumpy tapioca, but they remained professionally firm in following the doctor's orders.

"Nurse?" I knew that she knew what I wanted.

"Yes." She almost sung the word and walked from the nurses' station to my bed.

"Nurse, I can't swallow another ice chip. I've eaten a truckload already. Please, have mercy. I think I'm going into withdrawal, so how about calling McDonald's and seeing if they will deliver a hamburger, french fries—don't forget the salt—and a strawberry shake?"

She laughed. But I was serious.

"Don't you know," she began to instruct, "that you're getting all the nourishment your body needs through this little tube?" She pointed to the tube that ran from a bottle hanging above my bed down to a needle inserted in a vein in my hand. "It's called intravenous feeding."

"But I'm starving! And that's so boring!" I whined and rolled my eyes in the direction of the tube. My stomach agreed.

"Sorry. That's all for now." She patted my arm. "And don't worry; you're not starving."

The next day I was put on a liquid diet. I still remember how my taste buds cheered at the entrance of cherry Jell-O and cold lime sherbet. I endured hot, clear bouillon, which I had never liked. But after a few days of everything sliding down my throat without a single chew, the joy of Jell-O dwindled to "oh no, not again!" There wasn't "always room for Jell-O."

"Just because I'm bald and strung up by an ice tong, don't think my jaws don't work," I repeatedly informed the nurses. "Please, can't I have some solid food?"

"We can't; it's not on your chart. Besides, you might get sick, vomit, and choke," one nurse insisted.

"But you don't understand. I never get sick. I haven't thrown up in ages." My persistence got me nowhere; they were persistent right back. But they were gentle with me, and I couldn't be mad at them no matter how hungry I got, because I knew they were following instructions. I also knew that I was starving to death.

My first hospital meal was the aesthetic equivalent of pheasant under glass. A nurse cut the food into baby-sized bites and forked it into my mouth. I was like a baby bird, lying there, mouth open, anxiously waiting for those little bites. Chewing those bites brought a thrill of power—grinding, mashing, chomping the food into a mushy pulp before swallowing. I don't remember what kind of meat it was, only that it was substantial, solid food!

Eight days after my admittance, I was moved out of ICU up to the fourth floor, east wing. Two nurses and my parents transported me up on the elevator, and I was glad to be on my back so I could see where I was going. The normal hospital bed had been removed so my Stryker could be moved in; and in the semiprivate room, they locked the Stryker's wheels next to the window. For the first time in eight days I saw natural light. The brightness was majestic. The Intensive Care Unit had been on ground level, and I don't remember the shades ever being drawn in the eight-bed ward. I was not near a window and felt as if I were surrounded by a cloud the sun could not conquer. Only muffled light had filtered through. This light was a glorious, shining promise.

The hospital visiting hours allowed my parents to stay from six until eight, a time we spent laughing and talking and watching my roommate's television, the first television I had seen since I'd been in the hospital. Saying good-bye to them that night was difficult, but Mom said that she would see me in the morning.

Since my room was at the end of the hallway and right next to the elevator, I listened for the ding-ding of the elevator doors as they opened and closed, carrying not only my parents, but also other visitors, down to the lobby. Soon the dinging stopped, and the quietness magnified my isolation. Loneliness and pain triggered an explosion of tears; I couldn't stop crying. I cried more in self-pity than I had since I had been injured, and the more I cried, the more the pain pulled through my head and neck. I cried in helplessness and frustration, because I could not call a nurse to ask for a painkiller; in order to call a nurse, I had to push a button that rang in the nurses' station down the hall. And as much as my pride fought against the words, *I can't,* as much as my mind demanded, my arms and hands would not move toward the button. No nurses could hear my whisperings or my sobs as they had in Intensive Care.

The pain became like a vise, and its tightening bored deeper and deeper. The rush of tears narrowed to a stream of quiet sobbings as time seemed to stop, surrendering me to the darkness and the pain.

Lord, please, please, I prayed, *let me sleep.* I tried to shift my mind away from the pain and the situation and into imagining Jesus coming toward me, as I had seen in my dream the night I had been hurt. That dream became a mental panacea for many stabs of self-pity and loneliness. My well of tears dried, and my body stilled; sleep pulled over me like a warm comforter. God gave me rest.

The muted light from the hallway and the sound of the nurses as they strapped the Stryker Frames together pulled me out of my sleep. Feeling less pain, I uttered a thanksgiving. Every two hours throughout the night, although I would sleep through the strapping in, the flipping would jar me awake; the night seemed endless. I told time by counting the flips; it was four o'clock when the pain returned. Staring at the tiled floor till my eyes burned, I watched the morning light spill across the flecked pattern. To keep from crying, I tried to focus on one single fleck, the triangular one in the corner of the tile, the one about an inch away from the wall. But the tears came, and the one fleck became lost in a blur of frustration and fatigue. The mental pain of utter helplessness was as deep as the physical suffering. With more tears came more head throbs; I squeezed my eyes shut, and with each throb my heart cried, *Jesus.* I kept my eyes tight, thinking the power of sleep would unchain me from the pain, freeing me, if only for a short while; but sleep was not to be my liberator that night.

"Jama?" came a whisper that startled me back to reality. My tightened eyes ached as they popped open. The tile was brighter with morning light, and a pair of white nurse's shoes stood beside the bed. "Jama, do you want a shot for pain before we turn you?"

I fought to control my yes, but it was muffled in sobs.

After the shot was administered and I was flipped from stomach to back, I stared at the ceiling tiles and waited for the pain to dull until there was nothing—no feeling, no pain, no movement. And there were no more tears; all was stillness and paralysis. I closed my eyes and pictured Jesus; sleep came.

When I awoke again, the room was ceiling high with summer brightness. The pain was but an echo of what it had been during the night; it was bearable.

"Ma'am, could you please open the curtain?" I asked the nurse when she brought in the breakfast tray. "I want to see outside."

"Sure. It's a beautiful day." She pulled the nylon cord and the sun triumphed through the window. Just then Mom walked in.

"Oh, Mom! I'm so glad to see you!" I said with joy as she bent over and kissed my cheek.

"Your official breakfast feeder is here right on time, I see." She nodded toward the tray. "So how was your first night out of Intensive Care?"

While she spooned me the semiwarm oatmeal, I told her about the night and the frustration of not being able to push the button to call a nurse when I needed a pain shot.

"I guess no one thought about that," she replied. "I'll be right back." She dabbed the napkin on my mouth and left the room. When she returned from the nurses' station, she held in her right hand a small bell, the kind I had seen at a hotel desk. "One of the nurses gave me this. She said that when you need someone all you have to do is ding this bell."

The bell was placed on the right arm board about forty degrees away from my hand, and if I swung my arm in the right direction and at the right height, I could ding the bell. Mom stood outside the door to test whether it would be loud enough. She could hear it directly outside the room, but I was too far down the hall for the nurses to hear it. Mom went down to talk to them again.

"They'll make arrangements to move you across from the station tomorrow. That way they'll be able to hear your bell," Mom told me.

In one night I had made progress of a sort; I had new adjustments. I had been promoted from ICU to "please come when I ding." It wasn't much, but it was a beginning.

3

Little Changes

Her immediate beauty was her smile, because it pulled everything about her together, leaving one celestial image. Her smile unfurled a banner of joy from her face; her sporting smile made a victory team of her eyes and cheeks and mouth. She was my new roommate.

Sitting on the edge of the bed wearing a yellow houserobe, she didn't look sick, and I wondered why she was in the hospital. She couldn't have been more than a couple of years older than I was. The wonder was reciprocated. Curiosity lit her dark eyes, and she did a double take at my contraption.

After the nurses parked the Stryker in bed number one, closest to the door, I turned my head to the left and saw her bright smile again. The chasm that separates one from another was bridged by that smile. I smiled in return.

"Hi! I'm Karen." Her voice was timid, yet animated with cheer.

I stiffled the urge to be the comedian and blurt out, "Hi! I'm bald!" Instead, I responded demurely, "Hi! My name's Jama."

We spent the morning talking about our backgrounds. I told her of my accident, and she told me of her parathyroid operation. She pulsated with a love for life, infusing the hospital room with vigor and warmth. Her personality was joyous, and she was sensitive to my condition. She seemed much older than her fifteen years; no pity was in her eyes, only concern.

For the two and a half weeks that she was in the hospital, our room was seldom quiet. Our parents came three times a day, and in between their visits—and sometimes during their visits—we joked with each other, we mocked silly game shows, we sang along with the radio. We thought our singing was melodious, but a few wisecracking nurses had the nerve to call it "noise" and "racket." We also had visitors. Because of Karen's popularity in her high school and the report of my accident in the newspapers, there were many afternoons when there was standing room only. More than once a nurse had to inform us, "This is a hospital, not a party."

A day or two after I had been out of Intensive Care, Dr. Goodell called Mom to explain my prognosis to her. She was upstairs in her bedroom when the phone rang.

"Mrs. Kehoe, this is Dr. Goodell."

"Yes, how are you?"

"I'm fine, but I want to explain Jama's condition to you, and I wish that what I had to say was more promising. Because of the injury to Jama's spinal cord and the paralysis, she won't be able to roll over, sit up, or urinate and have normal bowel movements. She will need medication to soften her bowels and an enema every other day. She will also need a catheter, which will have to be changed every so often. The cord damage was severe, and I wish I had better news. I'm sorry."

"Thank you for explaining."

"Good-bye, Mrs. Kehoe."

Mom hung up the phone and reached across the nightstand for a pad of paper; she wanted to write down what he had said so that my healing would be to God's glory when it was manifested. Then the paper gradually fell from her hand and she sat on the bed motionless, the reality of what he had said hitting her full force.

God, I never expected it to go this far, she prayed, *for the doctor to come out and say this. I was expecting him to say that Jama would be all right.* Tears trickled down her cheeks. She was on a high wire, the balance of her faith wavering dangerously over the precipice of despair.

No, she thought suddenly, regaining her balance. *No, I can't do this.* She wiped away the tears with the back of her hand.

Knowing that Dad was teaching a class at the university, Mom got in the car and drove the four blocks to Betty Klem's house. In the few previous years, Betty and John Klem had been my parents' spiritual best friends. As she told Betty what Dr. Goodell had said, the tears slowly fell down her cheeks again, but she didn't fall into despair. She only felt disappointment that he had said what he did.

"Well Barb, this is just going to be for God's greater glory. That was the word that the Lord gave you at the first and now that you know what her injury is, it will be to God's greater glory." Betty reached across the couch and hugged Mom.

"You're right. You're right." Mom pulled a Kleenex from her pocket and wiped her eyes. From then on, she knew, consciously and spiritually, that she had entered the ark of faith and had shut the door. And she never really gave the seriousness of my condition too much more thought, because she knew that I would be healed to God's glory.

When Dad came home from school that evening, Mom didn't break down and cry when she told him what Dr. Goodell had said. As Mom finished explaining, Dad shook his head.

"No, no. I'm not accepting that. I can either believe what he's saying is going to happen, or I can believe what God says. I'm going to believe God." He was not denying the reality of my injury; he knew it was true. But he knew that Jesus was the greater Truth. Had he accepted what Dr. Goodell had said as the final word concerning my condition, he probably would have slammed his hand in defiance and angry despair against the table. But he resisted. "No," he affirmed, "it's not going to be that way." He shook his head again and held Mom's hand.

"Honey, tomorrow when you go feed Jama breakfast and you see Dr. Goodell, you tell him that I want her started on a physical therapy program. I want her arms and legs to be limbered. I want us to do all we can to work with them." He reached out and hugged Mom close. "Lord, help us."

The next morning when Mom relayed Dad's message to Dr. Goodell, he was not very enthusiastic about the suggestion.

"I just don't know how much good it will do, Mrs. Kehoe," he said. "But I'll go ahead and order it if you want."

"Dr. Goodell, my husband is in physical education at Ball State and coaches football. He knows how important it is for the muscles to be exercised. We believe that God is continually working in Jama, and we want all that's possible to be done with her arms, her hands, and her legs." Mom's faith stood strong against the negative report of my condition.

"Okay. I'll have a therapist sent to her room." His voice lacked all enthusiasm.

When Dr. Bergwall came in on his morning round, he also talked to Mom about my situation. He took her outside the room, so I couldn't hear what she would finally tell me months later.

"It's really a shame," he told her, shaking his head. "She has such a good mind, and her body is useless. Mrs. Kehoe, I really think that you and your husband should think about sending Jama to a rehabilitation center so she can learn to deal with what has happened to her."

Mom shook her head and said nothing. She knew she would never do such a thing. But she didn't think badly of Dr. Bergwall for saying what he thought. She knew that he and Dr. Goodell were only saying what they saw, that medically, yes, I was paralyzed. However, she believed that God was changing that situation.

A couple of days later, a uniformed woman walked into the room just as Karen and I decided that it would be fun to turn on a soap opera, turn down the volume, and make up our own script. Since I wasn't to be turned for another hour, I thought she probably wanted to see Karen and not me. Looking straight at me, she asked, "Hi! Are you Jama?" She had mispronounced my name as most people do.

"Yes. But it's Jama, long *a.*"

"Oh, sorry. I'm Carol, the physical therapist your doctor ordered. He wants you to get some exercise, but I'll go easy on you today because your muscles will be tight. We need to get them stretched out and limber, loosen them up a bit."

"Sounds good." I glanced at Karen and winked. She was sitting casually on her bed; she grinned and winked back. People came in and out and could do just about anything to me. I couldn't rise and flee from their respiratory machines, their X-ray machines, their needles, and their other technical apparatuses.

"We'll do some arm exercises first. Just relax and let me loosen the muscles. It may hurt a little, so you tell me when it hurts too much."

She grasped my right arm, bent it at the elbow, stretched it perpendicular to my body, then pushed it back in to my side. I felt like a chicken flapping one wing. The motion hardly hurt; the pain was more like a strangely pleasant soreness, the soreness of dormant muscles gradually being aroused. She then held my wrist with one hand, my shoulder with the other, and started to raise my arm up and back over my head, like the reach-for-the-sky exercise I had done in elementary gym classes. When my arm was halfway above my body, a sudden violent pain wrenched and pulled in my shoulder—painful war of muscle against muscle.

"Ahh! Wait! Please, please! My arm doesn't go that way!" I wanted to jerk down my arm to stop the pain that ripped through my shoulder, the pain that stripped the laughter and smile from my face and filled my eyes with tears. Carol stopped extending the arm, laying it on the sheepskin-covered board.

"I won't force it any more today, but gradually we'll work on straightening it out all the way. Because the muscles haven't had any movement, they're tight. It'll hurt until they get stretched." She moved around to the left side; the pain was just as deep. I stifled a whimper.

"Now for the legs," she pulled down the sheet, revealing my faintly tanned legs. I watched her and sighed. They were disobedient, deaf to my brain's screams for movement, their once vigorous, noisy, athletic declarations muted. I closed my eyes; the contrast between past and present sharpened as I envisioned jumping and splashing into the lake at camp, running along the beach during our Florida vacation, walking for hours on a shopping spree with my aunt. While Carol pulled and stretched my unresponsive legs, I prayed away the enemy—futility. *Greater is he that is in me . . . ,* I remembered. My legs had no tightness, no resistance like the arms; the only muscle movement was the uncontrolled dance of spasticity.

Carol pulled and stretched my arms and legs every afternoon. Gradually, the shooting pains in my shoulders lessened as the muscles became more flexible. I gained more movement in my arms; dinging the bell became easier, and I could bend my wrists slightly upward. But my hands were still tight fists of contracted muscles. My fingers had to be pried open, only to curl back into a fist once released. I could not hold or grasp; all meals were fed to me.

But the Lord was faithful to give little sparks of healing to let our family know that He was continually working in my body. One afternoon I discovered that I had more mobility than I knew about, when an itching nose beckoned for relief. Twitching my nose like a rabbit devouring garden leaves was futile; the itch persisted. Grimacing and squeezing my eyes shut to block out the discomfort was futile; the itch persisted. The misery overtook my body, and I felt like I was one enormous itchy nose. Then my entire face began to itch: my cheeks, my chin, my forehead. I wanted to scream.

"Oh, my nose," I whined. My arms came to the rescue, sliding off the lambskin shelves, appearing before my eyes to rub my tormented nose with the backs of my hands. Fiercely, I rubbed my nose, my cheeks, around the head and chinpads. The relief was ecstasy. I, Jama, had conquered the itch!

To help with my finger mobility, Carol told Mom and Dad to massage each finger as often as possible, which they did. While we watched TV, Dad would dab hand lotion on the backs of my hands and rub it in gradually, between my fingers and on my palms. Often he would massage my feet next, with special lotion to soften the callouses on my toes and heels. Massaging became Dad's own ministry, and I could hear him quietly praying while he rubbed.

Arching my thumbs backward was the first sign that I was gaining some specific hand movement. When I showed Dr. Goodell and Dr. Bergwall, they stood beside the Stryker with broad grins and wide eyes. "Do it again. Do it again," they kept repeating, as if they couldn't believe their eyes.

"See how God's giving her improvements!" Mom almost shouted. Her eyes moved excitedly from my moving thumbs to the doctors' faces.

"Yes!" Dad agreed, then added, "and I think the therapy is helping too. Thanks for ordering it, Dr. Goodell."

Dr. Goodell nodded slightly, saying nothing. Then both doctors said good-bye. Dr. Bergwall patted my arm, "Keep up the good work. See you tomorrow."

When they had gone, Mom and Dad could contain their jubilant praises no longer. I know the nurses in the station must have heard them praising and thanking the Lord Jesus. They hugged each other, giggled, and kissed me; then they asked me to move my thumbs one more time.

After that, they urged me to show off what God had done for me to each different visitor who came in. They linked the prayer "Pray for Jama's hands" into many prayer chains. Mom had explained what the word *paralyzed* meant to eight-year-old Julee, so the day after she saw me move my thumbs, she brought me a purple yarn ball to squeeze, "to get your fingers strong, Jama." Dad had to put it in my hand, and at first, I could barely lift it because my hands were so weak. But after a few days, I was lifting it up and down like an expert weight lifter with his dumbbell. Julee smiled when she saw me lifting it, proud that she had given something that had helped me.

"There's nothing to this," I informed Dad as I pumped the ball up and down.

"Then try *squeezing* it for a change." He stopped my arm with his hand midway in a pump.

"Well," I said after struggling to make a dent in the yarn, "that may take a few more days."

And that's all it took. In fact, the yarn ball was already getting boring. I was soon pumping and squeezing it at the same time and with either hand. It was time to put aside the yarn ball and press on to something greater—an orange.

The first time my opened palm received the orange, my hand wouldn't budge. My arm wouldn't budge. Nothing budged.

"All right, Dad, who put the lead weight inside this orange?" He laughed. I grunted, thinking that my muscles might hear the grunts, since they were obviously ignoring my brain messages.

"Hey, Mom, just tell the boys that if they really want to get muscles, if they really want to build up their arms, they should start lifting oranges!" But that orange was like the yarn ball—the more I lifted it, the lighter it got. And soon, I was squeezing it, making it soft and juicy. The end of the orange lifting and squeezing came when I heaved the orange over my shoulder and it flew out of my hand, spattering on the wall behind me.

Steve then delivered a handball which was heavier and much harder to squeeze; I definitely couldn't splatter it against the wall, which delighted the nurses. I also got in hand and finger exercising when Al, a friend from the youth group who came to see me often, made me a battery-operated light switch which I could flip on and off. People would wait and watch for me to move my thumb an inch to flick that switch.

As I moved from the yarn ball to the light switch, with increasing arm and hand movement, progress reports were phoned to family and friends. Our prayers were being answered. My family was walking by faith, not by what our eyes told us. By faith, we saw me healed and normal again. In claiming and claiming, in standing and standing on His promises, I knew that God was working in my body. Every time that I was flipped onto my stomach, I read and reread the Scripture taped on the board under me: "With God nothing is impossible" (*see* Luke 1:37). All the members of my family had to learn to hang onto our joy while we were waiting and standing. God gave us special doses of humor as we joked about my bald head (I joked as much as anyone), or as we teased the nurses, even to the point of surprising them with a "whoopie cushion" when they came to sit and visit.

Some of the nurses must have wondered about our state of mind at times. In fact, once some friends overheard a few nurses talking, saying that the Kehoes were crazy because they were so happy, and what was wrong with Mrs. Kehoe, didn't she love her daughter because she didn't cry or anything and she was always smiling. And they're always blessing the food and thanking the Lord for healing their daughter; well, couldn't they see that their daughter was paralyzed and she couldn't move? Why were they like that?

We were like that because we knew that God is God and that

He was working. Some nurses accepted, or at least tolerated, our attitudes and beliefs; we didn't try to hide our faith. But whatever they thought about us, we became friends with the nurses: Dad teased them; I sent some of the candy I received home with them to their kids; Julee went into the nurses' station to visit with them —they thought she was adorable and gave her orange juice and sherbet—no wonder she loved to come with Mom and Dad.

Sundays were usually our family days, days when we were all together and would sometimes become a little silly, the poor nurses receiving the results of our silliness. Sundays would begin with Dad and Julee bringing doughnuts to my room before the family went to church; then after they went to church and had eaten, they would come back with my portion of Mom's home-cooked meal, usually delicious pot roast, mashed potatoes, and corn. The nurses feigned great disappointment when I wouldn't share with them. It wasn't all feigned: The hospital food in no way compared with Mom's. After feeding me and visiting for a while, they would go home, just about the time that the nurse flipped me on my stomach. During that time, I would listen to the football games and doze. Then, in the evening, the whole family would troop up to my room again, this time with freshly popped corn, our traditional Sunday evening meal. I was getting so I could even feed myself a few kernels.

We had all kinds of fun together. One Sunday night Mom decided that she was going to have a little fun with the nurses, too. She took the black wig that was sitting on a Styrofoam head on my bed stand and put it on over her blond curls. The wig had been sent by the man who had always cut my hair, after Mom had told him that I had had my head shaved. But because of the tongs, I couldn't wear it just yet.

After the wig was in place, Mom bit her lip slightly to keep from smiling, then sneaked out of the room across to the nurses' station. In a serious voice she asked for directions to "Jama Kehoe's room." She just knew that they wouldn't recognize her with the wig on. And they didn't!

"It's room 426, right over there," a nurse said pointing.

Then Mom couldn't maintain the straight face and burst out

laughing. The nurse turned and peered closely. "Why, Mrs. Kehoe, what happened to your hair?"

We had a good time teasing the nurses after that, bringing up the fact that they didn't recognize a woman they had been seeing every day for months.

More often than not, when my family or when visitors were in my room, it was filled with laughter and joking. I made everyone who came in for the first time sign a pink, blow-up, autograph dog that had been one of my first gifts. Betty Klem had aptly named him "Smilin' Stryker," and Mom had taped him so that he hung from the long bar above the Stryker.

One day when Betty came to feed me lunch, we got into a goofy mood, and she decided that "Smilin' " needed a little clothing since autumn was on its way. Taking a napkin from the tray, she fastened it around the pink dachshund, diaper fashion. I laughed so hard watching her that I thought I would pop my tongs.

My spirits were encouraged when Mom and Dad or friends were with me. Saying good-bye to them was never easy. For Mom and Dad, too, leaving me alone in the night as they went back home was a time when the joking stopped and their faces were all seriousness. It was then that my tears came all too easily.

4

From Stryker to Bed

The days on the Stryker rolled into each other, and I wondered whether I would ever be freed of the tongs and the flippings. Finally, on October 27, the tongs were removed, and Dr. Goodell, Dr. Bergwall, and a nurse moved me from the Stryker to a regular hospital bed. A cervical collar was placed around my neck. I was to lie on each side for two hours at a time to lessen the possibility of bedsores, but at first I couldn't tolerate my body pressure on my arm and side. The collar was also very uncomfortable, rubbing against my chin and chest. Becoming adjusted to the bed and the collar took me a few days, but even the discomfort of the bed was better than being flipped on the Stryker. Because now I knew that if God wanted, He could heal me totally, and I could sit up and get out of bed since I wasn't strung up by the tongs. The progress from Stryker to bed gave my faith a boost, and I fully expected that one morning I would wake up and my body would be completely restored. My faith was childlike in anticipation.

A few mornings after I had been moved, the autumn light sifted through the slits of the white venetian blinds. My eyelids opened and closed with the slow, drowsy movement of a dreamer ushered carefully into consciousness. All was still except for the quiet, methodic breathing of my roommate behind the partially drawn curtain. I kept my eyes closed. With the rhythm, in the infancy of day, my mind drifted to the possibilities of the morning. Would this be the day? When I opened my eyes, would I see the resurrection of my paralyzed body? The vision of my jumping out of bed dissolved into a dream as I slipped back into sleep. But before the dream developed into anything more than that one image, a soft swishing pulled me away from the dream and into the light. I yawned with bedridden lethargy and opened my eyes. Peering through the guardrail, I saw Charlotte, one of the nurses, smiling at me.

"Good morning, Jama. How did you get on your side? Did someone come in to turn you? Your chart says that you're supposed to be on your back." Her eyebrows knitted together in question.

I was not awake enough to answer so many questions. "No one's been in to turn me. I guess I just rolled over in my sleep. I always used to sleep on my side. It sure feels a lot better than being on that Stryker." I buried my head deeper in the pillow.

"But are you *sure* a nurse didn't help you?" she asked again.

"No. I remember not wanting to wake up but wanting to be on my side, so I wiggled toward my left side as much as I could and then sort of pulled myself over with my right arm. I put my wrist against the guardrail to pull since I couldn't grab it with my hand. Then I went back to sleep."

"Well, that's great!" Her smile was broader than usual. "I'll have to tell Dr. Goodell. He'll want to know about this."

But Dr. Goodell wasn't nearly as excited as my parents—maybe he just didn't quite believe what had happened since he hadn't seen it. When I told Mom that I had rolled over by myself, she shouted, "Praise the Lord!" Charlotte's face was bright with joy as she watched Mom dance around and then give me a big kiss.

"I've got to call your father. I'll be right back. Charlotte, will you help her with her breakfast? I'll only be a minute."

"Sure, no problem."

Mom kissed me again and dashed from the room. Charlotte and I laughed. I didn't know that everyone would be so excited, but then I didn't know what they knew about my injury: Quadriplegics were not supposed to have the muscle control to roll over in bed by themselves. Mom didn't tell me what Dr. Goodell had told her about the extent of my spinal cord damage until months later.

Dad came to see me when his classes at the university were over, and he too kissed me and shouted his praise to God.

"I just knew that as soon as you got off the Stryker, God was going to start moving in you more rapidly. I've been expecting to hear news like this! I know that God is working in you!"

And the Lord continued His sparks of healing in my body. Little by little, I discovered more that I could do with the arm movements God was restoring. Bathing myself was one important improvement. It was birdbath fashion out of a blue plastic basin, but I could grip the washcloth with my thumb and, using my fist as pressure, rub the washcloth lightly over the upper part of my body. Charlotte would then help scrub my legs and toes.

Doing morning toiletries myself took extra time, but my self-esteem was lifted in knowing that I wasn't as dependent as I had been, that I didn't have to be cared for like a tiny baby. Even if I couldn't grasp the toothbrush with the strength of a nurse, my teeth seemed to feel cleaner when I brushed them myself. I still couldn't reach my arms up to wash my hair, but then there wasn't much to wash. Everyone teased that I had the "nubs," a beard's growth of four months on my head. But at least my hair was growing. When I had been completely bald, Steve had teased me by standing over my head, rubbing it solemnly, chanting, "Let me look into my crystal ball. . . ."

With each new improvement, fresh praises rang, and friends were quick to ask Mom or Dad, "What can Jama do now?" Even the nurses knew that God was doing something special in my life, and they began to encourage me to do as much for myself as I could. The little bell had been put in a drawer as I could now push the call button with my long thumbnail. And I didn't have to ring for the nurses to change the TV channels or turn the textbook pages for me, since I had gained more strength and movement in my arms and thumbs.

Charlotte was one nurse who became extra special. She worked the day shift, and every morning I looked for her happy smile. She had a gentleness and a compassion that made me feel hugged even when she wasn't touching me. I felt warm and comfortable when she was with me, because she talked to me and wanted to know more than how I was feeling physically to record on my chart; she wanted to know how my heart was feeling.

We had more than a nurse-patient relationship; we had a friendship. She brought her husband, her parents, and her sister to meet me; and my family, too, became her friends. I felt that Charlotte understood me—my pains, my frustrations, my odd sense of humor. Like all insecure teenagers, I had an overpowering need to be liked, liked for who I was. Charlotte's friendship was positive and uplifting, a gift from God.

But even with the improvements and the slow restoration of muscle movement, my attitude was not always one of praise and thanksgiving. I wanted my progress to be faster.

One morning in mid-November, after Mom had helped me with breakfast and Charlotte had helped me bathe and both had gone, melancholia covered me as I thought about all the days—which had now turned into months—that I had been in the hospital. I stared at the gifts which had accumulated in that time. Extra tables had been brought in and were covered with stuffed animals and plants. Banners and posters decorated the walls; mobiles hung from the ceiling.

As the sunlight warmed the room, I watched the mobile in the corner. The sun faces, colored with bright poster paint, turned and spun, and I remembered the last time that I had been out in the sun on that July day. Pain punctured my tender heart.

I had missed half the summer sun; I knew I would miss all the brightly painted autumn. Already it was November, and the chill of winter was in the air; my visitors had begun to wear their winter coats. The tan I had been so proud of had faded long ago. I looked anemic. "Like Casper the ghost," I joked. But those times I joked to keep from crying; inside, my heart hurt. *How much longer, Lord? How much longer in the hospital? How much longer until You heal me completely?*

I sighed deeply to calm away the knot of hurt. The faith of the morning became shadowed by sorrow. Turning my head toward the window, I felt the neckbrace rub against the rawness of my chin, the irritation adding to my mental aching. At that moment, more than anything else, I wanted to go home. I wanted to be back where I was at the beginning of the summer; I tried to pull my faith out from under the dark blanket of doubt, to believe that I would be as I had been. My eyes closed and released pent-up tears.

Streams of doubt and self-pity burned down my cheeks. I cried as I hadn't cried before. All the little steps of progress I had made were hidden in that darkness of unbelief. I couldn't praise God for squeezing the yarn ball, the orange, the handball, for picking up popcorn, for printing the alphabet, for grasping a fork, for the increased sensitivity and movement of limbs. I couldn't think of what I did have; I thought only of what I didn't have.

On the wall was a picture of me with a full head of hair that Mom had brought to show the nurses. I fought to keep from glancing at it. It was my cheerleading picture.

I had always wanted to be a cheerleader, but starting in the fifth grade, I had dedicated myself to improving my gymnastic skills and learning specific cheers. I wanted to have the best possible chance of making the junior high cheerleading squad. For hours I had stretched my muscles, gradually limbering them, then practiced and practiced the splits, the jumps, front and back walk-overs, handsprings, and roundoffs. I loved the feeling of flipping my body in the air and hearing the thud as my feet landed on the ground.

Auditioning in front of the seventh-grade student body and a panel of teachers had sent a nervous shudder through my body. Yet, I had the quiet confidence that I had the ability to be a good cheerleader. And I wanted a taste of the popularity and status that came with being a cheerleader; I wanted to be liked. I made the squad. The year brimmed with excitement and fun; I made new friends and cheered for a victorious basketball team. I wanted to be the best at everything I tried: I studied to make straight A's, wanting teacher and parent approval; I smiled to make new friends, wanting acceptance from my peers; I began gymnastic lessons, wanting to become a better cheerleader and gymnast.

I reveled in the pleasure and joy of my strong and athletic body. Spending so much time working out on the mats and trampolines at school, at the university on weekends, and at the gymnastic lessons, I knew that I was neglecting my growth as a Christian. Christianity was an important part of my life, but it was something that I took for granted, like the love from my parents.

In the future, I wanted to become a physical education teacher and have my own gymnastics school. After all, Dad was a football coach at Ball State, Mom had been a cheerleader, and both my brothers were athletes, playing almost every sport between the two of them. I had grown up catching footballs, dribbling basketballs, swinging baseball bats, teeing up golf balls, and running dashes—neither Steve nor Doug could catch me at tag. I couldn't imagine myself in a life without athletics.

My eyes tightened. The tears flooded in with the memory: the sight of arms swinging, hands clapping, legs moving; the sound of voices yelling, "Two bits, four bits, six bits, a dollar, all for the Spartans, stand up and holler!"

Now, in self-pitying despair, I wanted to cry out to God, "Why? Why did You let this happen to me?" The only thing that held me back from screaming in hot anger to the heavens was the Spirit strength in my foundation beliefs, an underlying hopefulness and faith that was supernatural. The weakness of the moment was the target. The fiery darts pierced, magnifying sounds and visions, worn Adidas pounding on a cinder track, water splashing after a somersault dive, tires squealing in a bicycle race. The enemy was hitting bull's-eyes; I cried from the blows. I could not hold the shield of faith.

"Oh, my God," my plea was a whisper. "Please give me something to hold onto. Help me believe. Help me believe. Jesus, heal me quickly, please." I had not cried in such need since the accident. I had cried in physical anguish for the elimination of pain, but this was a psychological need, an emotional need to be whole again. The physical pain had abated over the months; the mental pain had multiplied. My paralysis had become real.

I stared at my legs, shrouded in the white hospital sheets. "Why won't you move?" Silence. And then slight movement ruffled the sheets. Blinking in a double take, I reached for the button to raise the head of the bed, staring at the outline of my legs. "You moved, didn't you? Move again." I strained and forced the command downward. The sheet jerked up quickly and then was still. My heart pounded; I was short of breath, as if I had raced against the fastest runner in my gym class.

"What are you staring at?" It was Charlotte's voice. In my

concentration I hadn't heard her enter. "You're mighty deep in thought." She smiled.

"Charlotte, Charlotte, my leg moved! I told it to move and it moved! I saw it!" Every word was high-pitched in exclamation. But my joy didn't grab her as I thought it would. "Charlotte, didn't you hear me? My leg moved."

Her smile waned at the corners; her voice was quiet, the words fumbling. "Yes, I heard you. And that's good. But you know that it might have been just a spasm. You shouldn't get your hopes up when it could have been a muscle twitch."

"But it didn't feel the same as a spasm. I can't explain it, but it was different, like I had some control. It moved just a little, and even if it was a spasm, I know that my legs will be moving more." Her uncertainty could not arrest the uprising shield of faith inside me. I knew what I had prayed, and I knew the prayer had been answered. God was faithful. He came down and met me where I was. In my slipping hope, He boosted me, giving me something to hold onto: a sign that He was the Mover and that He would move in me.

Once more I turned my eyes to the daylight. *Lord, I'm hanging on. I'm trying to trust You, to believe. Please, just keep holding onto me and letting me know You love me.*

That sign of movement in my legs bounced me out of melancholy and onto a plateau of refreshed faith. The Thanksgiving holiday was approaching, and I indeed had a reason to be thankful: Dr. Goodell had granted me a leave of absence so I could spend the afternoon with my family at home! I didn't care that I could be away for only four hours; I was going home!

Thanksgiving Day as Charlotte was helping me bathe, I couldn't stop chattering I was so excited. She grinned and laughed and nodded, while I talked and talked about everything that was bumping around in my head.

"I'm so glad I'm working today so I can help you get ready and then see you off. I wouldn't have missed this for anything," Charlotte said as she sprinkled me with baby powder.

"Oh, Charlotte, I'm really glad you're here too!" I wanted to hug her because she was so dear to me.

Just then Mom entered carrying a sack and a new dress. I squealed with happiness.

"Oh, Mom, it's beautiful!" The dress was a light green, paisley pattern with a striped border around the bottom and around the long, angel-wing sleeves.

"I thought you'd like it." She smiled.

Mom and Charlotte helped me dress. Although I liked the dress, I hadn't worn clothes in four months, and it was slightly confining and uncomfortable. Then Mom slipped the black wig over my stubble and put some makeup base on my face. I felt as if I were going to a party!

Charlotte lifted me from the bed and sat me in the wheelchair. When my dress had been pulled down and my socks pulled up, Mom pushed me out into the corridor. Charlotte patted my shoulder and kissed my forehead.

"You have a great time, okay?" she said.

"You bet!"

"I'll be off work when you get back, so I'll see you tomorrow. Then I want to hear about everything."

"Okay. Bye!"

Mom wheeled me down to the emergency entrance where an ambulance was waiting to take me home. Friends from the university had chipped in to pay for the cost of the ambulance, because everyone was thrilled that I could go home and wanted to share in the blessing.

The ambulance ride took about fifteen minutes, and when we arrived all the relatives who had come were waiting with wide smiles as the paramedics brought me to the door. Once inside I was kissed and patted and hugged. My mind was swirling with all the activity and people.

So that I wouldn't have to sit up all afternoon, Dad had put pillows across one of our chaise longue chairs, and he lifted me into it. Although I was getting stronger, sitting up for more than an hour exhausted me.

Before being carted into the living room, I asked Mom if she would dial Christy's number so I could wish her a happy Thanksgiving. She did and held the receiver to my ear, knowing that I was unable to grasp it. Suddenly I was self-conscious about my hands, and I cut short the conversation because those around me were seeing my inability to open my fingers.

Since I was the center of attention, I didn't want everyone who looked at me to see how dependent I was. When dinner time came, and our plates were heaped with all the home-cooked dishes I loved, I ate very little because the fork kept falling out of my hand, and I was embarrassed to have Mom or Dad feed me.

I was relieved when dinner was over. I became more relaxed and just lay on the lounge chair laughing and joking with the grandparents, aunts, uncles, cousins, and everyone who came in and out of the living room. They hovered about me, asking repeatedly if I was comfortable or if I needed anything. I was content simply being in my home, seeing all the familiar pictures and furniture, seeing colors rather than hospital white.

But as the afternoon headed toward evening, the lounge became more and more uncomfortable. As much as I didn't want to admit it, I was ready to go back to the hospital to be in a comfortable bed. Exhaustion was sweeping through me.

The ambulance came to pick me up just as many of the men were ready for turkey sandwiches and reheated wild rice. Everyone crammed into the kitchen once more to say good-bye. I tried to be very brave and not let any tears slide from my eyes. My body was saying that I wanted to go; my heart was saying that I wanted to stay. The good-byes to Steve, Doug, and Julee were the hardest; love for them and for their presence filled me. I didn't want to think about the loneliness of that hospital room I was going back to.

As much as I regretted returning, I was still thankful that God had given me Thanksgiving at home. The loneliness and sadness that visited me when I went back to the hospital room could not oust the wonderful peace and praise that dwelt with me. As I lay in bed ready for sleep, I thanked God and prayed that the next time I went home I might be able to stay there for good.

5

A Hospital Christmas?

The hope and exhilaration of those early triumphs—turning over, brushing my teeth, sitting up—faded into black depression as Christmas approached. And then Christmas was a week away. A little, artificial Christmas tree adorned the table along the wall in front of my bed, displaying a touch of the Christmas spirit. And yet, the tree, so small, so artificial seemed strangely out of place in the hospital's "antisepticism." No green boughs, no tinsel, no mistletoe, no nativity—the little tree stood alone.

I felt no Christmas spirit. I felt alone. The weight of the sadness and loneliness was like a boulder on my heart. The afternoon was winter bleak; I was cold inside. I couldn't fight disappointment anymore. Each December day I had encouraged myself: *Soon, soon, I'll be leaving soon, I'll be home for Christmas.* Now those words had hollowed; I could pour in no more encouragement. Christmas was all I could think about. Christmas in the hospital. Christmas away from my family and my friends and my house. I thought of the decorations we put up every year and wondered if the house looked as beautiful and colorful as it always did during the Christmas season. I always thought our house was beautiful at Christmas, the prettiest one on the street.

The more self-centered I became, the more my disappointment deepened. Christ, the center of Christmas, became obscured by the choking weed of selfishness, the concentration on "me." Self-pity tightened around my faith. I couldn't pull the choking weed. I couldn't pray, and I couldn't think positively. I could only lie there and stare at the tree. I wanted to cry. I wanted to let the flood of tears break through the dam within me, to drown the choking weeds. I wanted to bury my head in the pillow, submitting to tears, the tears of an unhappy child.

My eyes burned from staring at the flashes of red, green, red, green of the Christmas tree bulbs, like the stop, go, stop, go of my tears. Closing my eyes, I sighed deeply over and over. Air entered; some of the tenseness escaped. I knew I had to move past the memories of hushed Christmas secrets, of wonders wrapped beneath a tree, of brisk sleigh rides on Christmas snow, of caroling around the neighborhood on cold, snowy nights. I knew I had to look past the memories, whatever they might be, and look to the baby Jesus of the manger, to the man Jesus of the cross, to the real meaning of Christmas. I rebuked my childish behavior.

"Hey, are you okay?" I had been so lost in my labyrinth of thought that I hadn't heard Charlotte come in the room. I jerked my head toward her, realizing that my eyebrows had been furrowed in concentration.

"Oh," I stammered for words, "I'm all right." She took a couple of steps closer to the bed. She knew I was stretching the truth. She always seemed to know when I tried to wall in my hurts and tears.

"Jama, what's the matter?" Her words were gentle, stroking my heart. She sat down on the edge of the bed and waited for my answer. I looked away and stared at the tree again. The battle against depression had fatigued my smile.

"I don't know, Charlotte. I guess I'm just sad. It's Christmas and I want to be with my family. It's just not fair. Why can't I go home?" I forgot about the rebuke I had given myself only minutes before. I heard the whining in my voice, the pouting childishness which my father scolded me about. I fought to hold back the tears. I still didn't want to look at Charlotte, although I could feel her eyes penetrating my sadness.

"Jama, listen." I turned and looked at her. "Now where's that sparkling smile I saw this morning when we talked about all the fun Christmases you'd had on your grandparents' farm? You were laughing when you told me about your uncle dressing up as Santa and taping on his mustache and its coming loose . . ."

"But Charlotte . . ." I interrupted.

"Wait a minute. I know it's hard. Nobody wants to be away

from home on Christmas. I know you want to be with your family. I want you to, too. And maybe you'll be able to. Remember you got to go home for Thanksgiving."

Guilt over my immaturity caused my eyes to lower from her glance. *You're such a baby, Jama,* I yelled at myself inside.

"Charlotte, I'm sorry. I know I shouldn't act this way. You're right. Dr. Goodell hasn't been in today; maybe when he comes he'll tell me I can go home. I'm okay now. Didn't mean to be a baby. You just caught me at the wrong time." I smiled and felt as if I'd climbed up a few notches closer to daylight. "And you know, I'd forgotten all about Thanksgiving."

"Hey, kiddo, you don't have to be sorry. We all get sad sometimes, but I just don't like to see you so down in the mouth." She smiled and winked. A trace of some secret seemed to glint behind the wink. Something in her eyes, the way they twinkled with sparks of mischief, gave me the feeling that she knew something very important, some "king-of-the-mountain" secret that she wasn't telling me.

"Yes, yes, I know. But why are you looking at me that way? What's up? Come on, you look like you're holding in something mighty important." I teased in hopes that she would let that cat I heard meowing out of the bag. "You can tell me," I whispered. "I won't tell."

No such luck.

"What are you talking about?" she said, turning her back to leave, knowing very well what I was talking about. Her abrupt behavior spoke loudly of some hidden knowledge. "I've got to get back on the floor now. I'll see you a little later. And I want you smiling when I come back, okay? No more frowns. You'll get awful wrinkles." She was out the door before I could utter another plea for information.

Rats, I thought. *What's going on? Maybe they're going to let me go home for Christmas Day like they did for Thanksgiving Day when Dr. Goodell had given me a "leave of absence" for four hours.* My thoughts began turning from the minuses of being in the hospital to the pluses of being able to go home. I was much stronger and more mobile than I had been six weeks earlier when

I got off the Stryker, or even a month earlier at Thanksgiving. I could sit in the wheelchair for longer periods of time, long enough so that Dr. Goodell had given his permission for me to go down to the lobby. The first trip down was a family affair. Julee pouted because she couldn't push me, but Dad had said that I was "too valuable a cargo." I smiled, feeling like royalty as they all escorted me down in the elevator and into the lobby.

My eyes were wide with wonder as I soaked in sights and sounds; the lobby was crowded with holiday visitors. Several people looked at us with curiosity since my head had only inch-long hairs, but I didn't feel embarrassed because I was so happy to be out of the hospital room. When I smiled at them, they feebly smiled back and turned their heads.

Steve, Doug, and Julee rattled on and on about getting out of school and about their choices of Christmas gifts. We laughed and teased each other about our greediness. Julee, for the first time, declared that she wanted more clothes than toys.

"Hey, Mom, look at that baby." Since I couldn't extend my finger to point, I nodded to my left in the direction of the baby. A year-old little girl was standing at the side of her mother's knee shaking a key ring loaded with keys. She dropped it suddenly, looked startled, then bent down to retrieve it. She giggled, and Mom and I smiled. Evidently liking the sound that dropping the keys made, she continued dropping and picking up the ring. I watched as her fingers extended and grasped the keys, then as they opened to let the keys fall.

"Mom, that baby is doing something I can't do. And she doesn't even know it." I didn't pity myself as much as I marveled at what a baby could do. I knew that God would take care of my hands.

"But you'll be picking up keys again before long," Mom replied. "They just better not be my car keys." Mom's implication was evident and I laughed. "God is wonderful, isn't He, Jama, to put such movement into that baby's tiny fingers?" She looked at the baby's hand and then at her own as she opened and closed it. "God gave us incredible bodies," she added. I nodded in agreement.

The visit to the lobby was followed by other journeys. Since I was able to travel via wheelchair, I also went down to the physical therapy department instead of Carol coming to me. She continued to give me range-of-motion exercises on my arms and legs, but now I was also put on a tilt table—a table that tilted my body at angles so that eventually I would be in an upright position. The table was to help decrease the lightheadedness I had from being on my back for so many months and to help me become accustomed to having the weight of my body on my feet.

Every time the angle was cranked up, the blood rushed downward from my head, and I just knew that I would throw up and faint. But I never did, and soon I was cranked to a standing position and staying there for almost thirty minutes. Carol asked Mom to bring some shoes to give me support, so Mom brought my favorite pair of tennies. I hadn't worn shoes for nearly five months. "You'd better get used to them," Mom said when I complained that they felt funny. "I'm not going to let you out of the house without them. Not in the winter anyway."

The months in the hospital hadn't changed Mom and Dad's faith that I would be healed. They saw the healing coming little by little, and their encouragement and trust in God boosted my sometimes feeble faith. Mom was usually with me when I went to therapy, so that I would have someone to talk to when I was strapped to the tilt table. Often, we watched the people passing by the window that was directly in front of the table. I noticed that the college girls who passed were wearing the new maxicoats.

"I think you'd look good in a red one, Jama, like that one there," Mom said one day, pointing to a petite girl walking down the sidewalk on the other side of the street. "It would surely keep your legs warm when you went to school." Her words were positive. In her mind she saw me walking to school in that red maxicoat.

After I finished the physical therapy program, I was started on a self-help program in Occupational Therapy across the hall. Even though I was practicing to do things which I knew I should do, I resisted the program. I just didn't like the idea of being forced to button and unbutton, type, and write with someone watching and recording what I was doing. My adolescent immaturity flared into rebellion. I wanted to do what *I* wanted to do when *I* wanted to do it. Much of my rebellion was caused by my frustration and awkwardness at not being able to do the simple tasks I had always been able to do before without thinking. I was embarrassed when my fingers would not do what I told them to do. I didn't like to be watched while I struggled. But later, when I was in my room, I laboriously worked at printing the letters of the alphabet.

. . . . never easy. They require a certain strength, a declaration of war . . . . ativism, a first step on the water. Beginnings are frustrating. . . . . s struggling with beginnings, and I was struggling with frustrations. I was beginning to put forth an effort to withdraw from my dependence on others, to do things for myself. I had begun to wash myself, and although I couldn't use a knife yet, I could feed myself. When Mom, Dad, and the kids came up with one of Mom's meals, I grasped the fork, mostly with the strength in my thumb, and ate with delight as we all watched "Gilligan's Island" and talked about the day. Often I had to rethink how to do things, remembering that I had use of only a limited number of muscles and movements. The right side of my body seemed to have more strength than my left: My right hand was stronger, and my right leg was less spastic. And because of the weakness of the left side, I had trouble holding a pencil since I was left-handed.

The day Mom brought a big fat pencil like the kind used in first grade, I thought that she was kidding.

"You mean you actually want me to *write* with that thing?"

"Well, it's big enough for you to grip, isn't it?"

She had a point. But I still protested. "But Mom, I'm *thirteen.* "

"But if it works, it works, right?" She smiled. I couldn't argue with her when she smiled.

I was trying to manipulate the pencil to find the position where I had the most finger pressure, when a young intern named Bob walked in.

"Hi. What's this action?" he asked, grinning, his eyes widening at the size of the pencil. I wanted to thrust it under the sheet in embarrassment. *Oh, why did Mom have to buy one that was fire-engine red?*

I laughed to cover the embarrassment. "Hey, don't laugh. I bet you had a pencil like this once, too!"

"I have a vague recollection of something similar." He laughed.

"Come back later and I'll show you how it works to refresh your memory," I promised.

"You've got a deal. See you in a while. I've got work to do."

I was on the Stryker at the time, so as soon as I was flipped on my stomach, I tried holding the pencil and working to print the letters of the alphabet. Only the largeness of the letters made them legible, they were so faint. After I had printed a few letters, my hand always became tired, and the pencil would fall out. When Bob came back, I showed him the notebook.

"Hey, that's not bad! But you're going to have to make those letters smaller. You're wasting too much paper. Tell you what, as soon as you can write my name in between two of these lines, I'll splurge and treat you to pizza and Cokes. But don't you dare tell the nurses!" He smiled at the offer, just the right incentive for a teenager. Pizza. My mouth watered.

"You've got yourself a bet!"

I let Charlotte in on the bet, making her promise not to tell anyone else. To help me practice, she would take my notebook and print the letters down the side. Then I would write each letter all the way across as many times as I could, writing as small as I could. At first, I had to use two lines for each letter, and each was so light it was barely visible. I had to rest after every line, the concentration was so tiring. The drive to succeed gave me power in my continual battles with frustration. I was winning more rounds than I was losing, but it took me more than a month before I triumphed. I not only wrote Bob's name once; I filled half the page with his name. I won the bet.

Writing in script had come next. "Teenagers don't print," Bob had said. Besides being promoted to script, I was also promoted from the school of the red pencil to the school of the ball point pen. As Christmas gifts for many of the people who had visited me, I signed my name, in script, on copies of a poem by Helen Steiner Rice called "Faith."

My wandering mind came back to the present, and I turned my head to look out the window, checking for snow. I had just finished signing those poems yesterday down in Occupational Therapy. I must have signed close to 50, but it had seemed like

500. *I've got more pluses on my side than I thought,* I told myself. The fog of depression was lifting. Light was slicing through. Maybe I could go home for Christmas Day.

Just as I was wondering if I should ask Dr. Goodell, he came walking in the room, garbed in a blue surgical uniform. He asked the usual questions, poked around in the usual places, while I responded with the usual answers. Then, suddenly, he was different. Dr. Goodell was grinning broadly, and he had that same twinkling in his eyes that Charlotte had had earlier. *I wonder if now's a good time to ask him,* I thought. But then he started talking about my progress in therapy, and the longer periods of time I was now able to spend in the wheelchair, and my increased mobility and reflexes. *Yes, yes, what else, what else,* I kept thinking, wanting him to get to the point that might solve the mystery behind everyone's odd behavior all day.

And then he stopped speaking. I watched him as he licked his lips and smiled again. My eyes ballooned with anticipation; I couldn't remember ever seeing Dr. Goodell smile like that. I wanted to scream, "Out with it! Out with it!"

"Jama, I am really pleased with your improvements. They're much more rapid than we had expected. And I think that maybe you've stayed here long enough. I think that your parents and family can take care of you at home as well as we can here. We're going to let you go home."

That last sentence floated in the air. My mind was numbed by the words. My ears heard them, but my mind was anesthetized to their meaning. I mumbled and fumbled for words of my own to question the meaning behind his words. Language was lost, as unattainable as reaching up to scoop a cup of cloud. I was afraid that what I had heard would not be truth. Finally, I formed the questions: "Are you serious? I can go home? I can really go home? And I can stay home? For good, and not come back?"

"Yes, yes, yes. I'm serious. You can. Not today, though. After the weekend, on the twentieth. The nurses will have to show your mother some procedures needed to take care of you."

"You're not kidding? I can stay? I don't have to come back after Christmas is over?" My eyes were wide as I rattled off my questions. He tilted his head back slightly, and I heard him softly chuckle.

"Jama, you *can* go home. And you *can* stay there. Of course, you'll have to come back for therapy during the week. And we'll have a nurse stop in to see you a couple of times those first few weeks to see if your mother has any problems."

"Oh, wow," was the extent of my vocabulary. So I said it again, "Oh, wow."

Dr. Goodell flushed, then regained his professional manner and moved toward the door to leave. "We're getting the necessary papers all ready for your parents to sign, and then on Monday you'll be released. I must get back to another patient. I'll see you tomorrow."

"Dr. Goodell?" My voice was quiet with deep emotion. "Thank you."

He turned at an angle, his profile shadowed by the light contrasts from hall to room. His response was barely audible. He seemed embarrassed and shyly nodded, still moving toward the door.

"Dr. Goodell?" I stopped him again. He waited but didn't turn around. "Merry Christmas!"

6

Grandpa's Bank

Big, fluffy flakes of snow fell on my head, my coat, my lap as Dad pushed my wheelchair from the entrance of Ball Memorial Hospital to our station wagon.

"Not so fast, Dad," I said, enjoying the snow, turning my face upward to receive the cold little kisses. I felt as if I were inside my grandmother's old, snow-filled paperweight that I used to turn upside down and shake. I was floating as free as the snowflakes. I was outside, breathing the winter air, looking up into the vast sky. I was near the trees and roads and not four stories up. To know that I was going home to stay filled me with praise and thanksgiving and love for God, my God who knows all the desires of the heart. I watched the snowflakes melt as they touched the warmth of my hands, and I couldn't keep from smiling. It was glorious to be going home.

When we arrived at the house, relatives were everywhere—aunts, uncles, cousins, grandparents, more than had been gathered on Thanksgiving. Christy even visited for a while. Our house was chaotic. But it was wonderful. Steve, Doug, and Julee took turns pushing me from room to room so I could see all the Christmas decorations. In each room people were smiling and coming over to hug me. They kept saying that I was their little Christmas present. I was wearing a new dress—the first time since Thanksgiving that I had worn clothes other than nightgowns—and I felt regal and very Christmasy.

Mom, Dad, and the boys carried in all the things I had accumulated over the last five months. Nobody knew where to put anything. Since my bedroom was on the second floor, Mom decided that whatever wasn't a necessary item, like my collection of stuffed animals or the pitcher collection that Aunt Billie had started for me, would go upstairs in my room. And whatever was necessary, like my nightgowns, lotion, and washbasin, would go downstairs in Steve's room. I loved my own room with my fuzzy pink carpet and all my china miniatures, and I wanted to go up and see it. But Steve's room was near all the activity, and I didn't want to miss a thing.

"Here you go, J. Sue," Dad said, using one of the many affectionate nicknames he had given me. He parked me in front of the fireplace where I could enjoy the warmth, plus see the Christmas tree. He reached down and kissed me. Deep inside I wanted to give him a big hug, but I couldn't make my arms move high enough to reach around his neck.

"I love you, Daddy." I looked into his eyes. "It's so good to be home."

"And I praise God that you're finally here, honey." He gave me another kiss.

All the excitement soon wore me out. I didn't want to go lie down, but I knew that if I was going to get up again to eat the evening meal with my family, I had to get some rest. Mom helped me undress and put a robe on me. Then Dad lifted me like a fragile china doll into Steve's bed. I didn't think I would be able to fall asleep because of all the noise, but a tender wave of drowsiness washed over me. I yawned, closed my eyes, and fell asleep, thanking God.

A few days after I had gotten home, Grandpa Kehoe came into the living room where I was watching television with Steve, Doug, and Julee. We were laughing at the commercials and wondering what we would be getting inside the wrapped packages under the tree.

"Hi, Grandpa. What's up?" I asked. He had something in his hand, holding it slightly behind his back.

"Remember this?" He held out the small cedar bank that he had given me shortly after I entered the hospital. I smiled and sighed inside; I knew what was coming. When Dad had told Grandpa that I had lost almost all movement in my hands and fingers, he knew that if I wanted to make those muscles strong again, I would have to exercise them. So when he brought me the bank, he made a deal with me. To motivate me to improve my digital dexterity, he said that if I could open that bank by putting the little key into the lock and turning it, he would put a twenty-dollar bill in it as a reward.

I had gotten only one other twenty-dollar bill in my whole life, and I had enjoyed that feeling of wealth, so I was not about to let such a generous offer pass. I had practiced off and on while in the hospital, but the key was so small that it kept falling out of my hand. It was frustrating; even my stronger right hand couldn't grasp it. My finger movements had greatly improved since those first days in Intensive Care when my hands were so knotted that it took most of the nurse's strength to pry them open. Now I could pick up popcorn and potato chips, turn pages of a book, hold a spoon and fork, and write with an ink pen. But I had yet to succeed in the finer movements of operating the bank key.

"Sure I remember that, Grandpa." I smiled. "How could I forget a bet, especially when twenty dollars is concerned!"

"Okay, then, let's give this thing a go. My wallet has an extra twenty in it just waiting to get inside this bank." He sat down on the edge of the couch and put the bank in my lap. "Here, let me put the key in your hand to get you started. And I'll hold the bank so it won't move while you're sticking the key in the lock." I saw the look in his eyes as he slid the tiny key between my thumb and my index finger. I think he wanted me to succeed even more than I did. His look was not of pity, but of deep compassion, authentic grandfatherly love.

"Yes," I agreed. "You help me get started, and I know I'll soon be twenty dollars richer. I need the money, Grandpa. I still have Christmas presents to buy. Okay, I've got the key. Now left fingers, you guys grab onto that lock," I commanded my hand, reaching for the small lock. The tricky part of the operation was keeping my hands steady enough to place the key deeply into the lock and still retain enough strength and pressure in my fingers to turn the key and open the lock. I had been able to get the key into the lock before, but never all the way in, and never with enough reserve strength to turn the key. I waited to hear the lock click as I had waited for the chimes on the ice cream truck when I was small. This click, however, was much more important.

Okay, Jama, I told myself, *now's the time, now's the time.* Concentrating, I blocked out the noise from the television, the clatter in the kitchen, the steady drone of conversation throughout the house. I focused all my mind energy and finger energy on lock and key. But they were more than lock and key. Grasping and successfully manipulating them was movement, it was crossing a bridge over the chasm separating paralysis from movement. I sucked in my breath and sent up a prayer.

I heard the click. I turned the key back to the original position, but hearing the sound had drained the strength from me. I couldn't pull the key out of the lock.

"Grandpa, it's open," I exclaimed, knowing he, too, had heard the click of victory. "Look, it's open." I turned the bar on the lock and slipped it off the latch; the key was still dangling from the lock. I felt as if I had just crossed a finish line, breaking the tape, sweating, exhausted, jubilant in victory.

"You did it, you really did it, by gum." His smile went from one white sideburn to the other. He reached over and patted my hands, which still held the bank and the lock. Then he leaned over the wheelchair and hugged me. Moistness crept into the corners of his eyes, and becoming a little embarrassed at his own emotions, he stuttered, "I-I-I-I have to go tell your father. I'll be right back." He stood up to leave, but halfway to the door he turned. "Oh, yes, your money, your money. Almost forgot." I had to smile at his absentmindedness. I loved him and wanted to hug him again.

He stood beside the wheelchair, reached into his wallet, pulled out the twenty, and triumphantly deposited it into the open cavity of the bank. "It should have been a hundred for what you just did," I heard him mumble as he left the room to find Dad.

"That was really good, Jama," Steve said. I had forgotten they were in the room watching my little performance. Pride was in his eyes and his smile. Doug and Julee were silent, but nodded and grinned in agreement.

"Thanks. Praise the Lord, huh?" I sighed. I stared down at my hands. Slipping the lock through the latch, I pressed the bar that bolted it secure.

One more victory!

7

Step by Step

The little victories kept coming.

After Christmas when the relatives had left, my family adjusted to a routine scheduled around my care. Mom became "nurse." The nurses at the hospital had given her a crash course. She did well with everything, except the enemas. Mom just couldn't manage the enemas that the doctor had said I needed every other day.

"Okay, Jama," she said, walking into the bedroom. Three times that day she had tried unsuccessfully to give me one. We were both frustrated, and yet, when she sat down on the bed, we started laughing. She shook her head. "I guess God didn't create me to be a nurse."

"I guess not," I answered. "Nor me to be a patient."

"Well, that's the last enema I'm going to give you."

"You mean *try* to give me, don't you?" I laughed.

"Very funny." She nudged me. "We're just going to have to trust God in this matter, okay?" She didn't have to persuade me. I hated enemas.

So we trusted. And God was faithful. We waited and won the battle. I never had another enema.

We decided to continue exercising our faith and trust God for the control of my bladder. I wanted the catheter removed. For several weeks before I had left the hospital, it had bothered me. It began leaking and had to be changed often. The nurses wouldn't believe me when I told them that I could *feel* it leaking, because they knew that quadriplegics were supposed to have no sensitivity as well as no muscle control. But God was restoring my sensory responses and I knew it! I was feeling the uncomfortable leaking.

When Mom called Dr. Goodell to tell him that she wanted the catheter removed, he adamantly opposed the decision. He knew the medical complications possible if the bladder of a paralyzed person becomes full and the urine isn't released. Even when the person has a catheter, it has to be carefully watched for clogging or malfunctioning. When the bladder becomes full and is not emptied, the nervous system responds with increased action of the reflexes, causing severe hypertension, or very high blood pressure. This is a crisis situation, which could result in death if the bladder is not emptied and the blood pressure lowered.

But Mom didn't know all the medical complications. She just knew that we had to trust God for His healing in every part of my body.

"We're going to trust God, Dr. Goodell," she told him over the phone.

"Mrs. Kehoe, I don't advise this."

"Well, thank you, Dr. Goodell, but we're still going to trust God. Jama says that she has feeling and that the catheter really bothers her. We believe this to be God's message that He's doing something for her."

And trust we did. The trusting was day by day after one of the nurses came to the house and removed the catheter. Although I knew when I had to void, I had no muscle control to hold it in. When I shouted, "Hey Mom!" she knew to come running. But we were on our way up. The roots of our faith were going deep into God as our only source for life and health. With each little victory, every member of the family rejoiced, our spirits going higher unto Him. As a family we were being drawn together in a tight bond of love. There was no embarrassment about sharing the healings that God was performing in my body. It was normal for humans to go to the bathroom, and we had prayed for my body to be completely normal again. Even eight-year-old Julee understood that. Until my muscles became stronger, Mom had to be within calling distance, or else I would have an accident.

"How would it be if your mother and I went over to some friends' house for a while tonight?" Dad asked as he lifted me from the wheelchair into the bed. "I think Mom needs to get out of the house. We won't be gone long, and if you need us the boys can call and we'll be right home." It was the first time that they had both been out of the house at the same time since I had come home.

"I'll be fine," I told them as they kissed me good-bye. My smile was weak; I hoped that I wouldn't have to go to the bathroom while they were away. I did. The pressure increased. I closed my eyes and waited for them to return home. They didn't make it in time.

Later, lying in the bed on fresh linen, I stared at the ceiling and wondered how long I would remain in my baby dependent condition. I knew I had interrupted my parents' evening, and I knew that I was a tremendous burden on them. I couldn't understand what God was doing. My eyes were sore and puffy from tears. I felt the silence of the night and my heart ached.

Gradually my strength increased. If Mom helped me to the bathroom before she left the house, then she wasn't concerned that I might have an accident while she was gone. And I became less worried too. However, when I was left sitting up in the wheelchair, Mom *was* concerned about the muscle spasms. Muscle spasms, or even a sudden sneeze, would jerk my body with a force that would topple me out of the wheelchair onto the floor. I lacked the strength to hold onto the arms of the chair.

But we had to keep trusting, and my parents believed that when I was left alone in the house I would be kept safe. One night Dad wanted to take Mom to a Ball State basketball game. Steve, Doug, and Julee were going with their friends, and Mom wasn't so sure she should leave me alone for the few hours that they would be gone. I heard them whispering in the front foyer next to the living room where I was sitting, watching television.

"Hey, you guys, you'll miss the game if you don't hurry. If you'll change the channel before you go, I'll be just fine and dandy." I heard the heels of Mom's shoes click on the linoleum floor.

"Okay. I'll get you some potato chips before we go. We'll be home as *soon* as the game is over."

"Mom, really, I'll be all right." I told her firmly. *I may have to be helped like a baby right now, but don't treat me like one,* I wanted to tell her. I depended on her, yet a healthy balance of dependency had to be established between us. The letting go had to come, even if it were little by little. To have things done for me was more convenient than to wait, to struggle, to labor, attempting to do them myself.

Cutting my food at the dinner table was a battle fought at almost every meal. At first I tried the easy foods: hamburger, spaghetti, tender pot roast. But sometimes the meat would slide away from my fork, running into the vegetables, sending peas or corn across the table.

"Oh, Mom, I'm sorry," I apologized one night when my pot roast pushed into the potatoes, spilling gravy all over the table-cloth.

"That's okay; I'll just wipe it up. Here, let me cut that for you." Mom was sitting beside me and reached over with her knife and fork toward my meat.

"Barbara, leave her alone. She can do it," Dad said eating a bite of potatoes. Dad always seemed to be the one who was determined that I could do something, like cutting my food or opening my mail, if I would only give it my best try. And if I didn't do it the first time, that didn't mean that I couldn't ever do it, but only that I would have to keep trying, and eventually I'd get it done. Mom had always had a protective heart; she wanted to protect me from the frustrating struggles, the embarrassment, and the hurt. Within her there was a prayer to God, *You could touch her right now and that wouldn't be so hard for her.* But intermingled with her prayer was a joyous praise in her heart for what God had already done in my life, that I was sitting there with the family, holding a fork, intensely working at separating the meat into bites.

I wanted my progress to be visible so, although cutting my food, writing out my homework, inching my way along in the wheel-chair were daily battles fought with clenched, tight fingers, feeble weak muscles, and fettered nerves, I kept trying and trying. They were battles of the soul, battles which caused me to grow in faith. And with the little victories—like slowly sawing into a pork chop with a knife—came proclamations of God's continuous healing power. Faith was made stronger, fed and nourished by the visible works of His hands. As frustratingly slow as the improvements seemed at times, they were coming. My muscles were becoming stronger.

I wasn't just gaining strength in my hands, but also in my legs: I had taken my first steps along the parallel bars in therapy. I had strained and concentrated so much that after the length of the bars I was exhausted. But they were steps, no matter how long it had taken me to go the distance of the bars. Dad had been with me when I had taken them. I saw his heart in his eyes: praise God.

The next day Dad came home with a walker. He brought it into the living room where we were all watching television. "Okay, everybody watch. Now you'll see how strong Jama's getting." He set the walker down in front of me and flipped up the footrests; my short legs didn't touch the floor. I looked down at my legs. I looked at the walker. My family looked at me.

I sighed. *Okay, Lord,* I thought, *for my family.* After locking the chair so I wouldn't move backward when I pushed up from the armrests, I positioned my hands on the edge of the arms, my elbows jutting out like chicken wings. "Well, here goes," I said.

"Thank You, Jesus," I heard my mother mutter. Three sets of eyes from the boys and Julee watched my movements.

Taking a deep breath, I leaned forward a little in the wheelchair and fixed every fiber, every thought, every bit of energy within me on the image of Christ. Now was the time; I paused. I stared at the blueness of the carpet at my feet. I blocked out sounds and forms. I thought of Jesus. With all the energy I had in me, I pushed down on the arms of the chair to lift my body up from the seat. My feet touched the ground, and my body raised about halfway up. I tried to adjust my feeble grip to get better leverage, but my strength evaporated; I sank back down in the chair. My spirit sank a little, too, feeling a dart of defeat.

"Hey, that's pretty good, Jama!" Dad encouraged. "You couldn't even lift your little rump before. Here, let me get you up, and then I think you can use the walker just like you used the parallel bars the other day. Up we go," he said, standing in front of me and lifting me up under the arms. When I had gotten my balance, a very teetering stance, Dad opened my hands and placed them on the grips of the walker.

"Don't let go, Dad."

"I'm right here. I'll be behind you," he said. "Barb, stand along here beside her." Mom had been standing by the couch and was beside me before I saw her take a step. I readjusted my hands on the grips and looked down at my legs again. Everyone was quiet, too quiet. It made me nervous.

"Feels kind of nice to be five feet two again," I joked. "Now, I'm taller than you again, Mom." I looked her in the eyes while she stood beside me. She laughed.

"When are you going to show us your stuff, Jama? We've seen you stand before." Steve commented from the couch.

"My stuff is coming up." I lifted the walker and set it back down a few inches farther ahead of me; then I slid my right foot forward and then my left. My brain shouted orders to my feet. Gripping the handles more tightly, feeling the moistness of perspiration against my palms, I wanted to pick up the walker and throw it away, running freely and unshackled. But I moved slowly forward.

"I'm getting tired, Dad."

"Steve, unlock the wheelchair and wheel it up behind her." He nodded in Steve's direction as he remained behind me. He had taken his hands away. Now it was me and the walker—and Jesus. "Jama, when you think you've gone as far as you can, Steve will have the chair and you can just sit down."

"Okay. Thanks, Steve." I moved forward again after stopping to take a deep breath. Little, tiny, baby steps shuffled me along the carpet. I pulled my legs forward at the hips, my arms receiving much of the weight by forcing down on the frame of the walker. All my concentration was on picking up my feet. I knew I should be praying, but I couldn't talk and walk at the same time. *Lord, I'm thinking of You!* The message shouted from my heart while I rested again. One more, two more, three more steps.

"Okay, Steve," I gasped, feeling the strength ooze from me, my knees lowering. The seat of the wheelchair was under me as I collapsed.

Practicing walking with the walker during commercials and after school helped to strengthen my arm muscles, and soon I was able to lift my body from the chair to an upright position. Not every effort was successful, however. As my crouched body would struggle to stand straight, I would often waver and fall back into the chair. "Lord, Lord, Lord," was all I could mutter through clenched teeth as I concentrated; and when I would lose my balance and fall, the prayer became "Please, please, please Lord." Failure was exasperating; but then, I wouldn't know success unless I kept at it. And as spring turned to summer, my weakness turned into strength: I began rising more times than falling. Someone always stood beside me in case a muscle spasm jerked me off balance; but the spasms were also becoming less frequent.

As soon as the spring weather was warm enough, Dad decided that I needed some outdoor exercise. Our family had always been so athletic that even my being in a wheelchair didn't stop us from enjoying sports together. The only difference now was that we just had a few more restrictions. One Sunday afternoon, we all piled into the station wagon and went over to the Ball State tennis courts behind the gym. Dad helped me into the wheelchair when we arrived and pushed me over to the back of the building. Opening my clenched hand, Dad helped me grip the tennis racket.

"Okay, Jama, now you swing at the balls when I bounce them off the wall. Watch your form now," he teased as he tossed the ball. I whiffed it; the tennis racket wobbled and fell out of my hand.

"Oops," I laughed.

"Now how are you going to hit the balls without a racket," Steve said, laughing. He and Doug were volleying two balls across the net.

"Very funny, Steve. You don't know, maybe I can." We were giggling and having a good time. I felt no self-pity that I could not be racing around the court after balls. Instead, I felt great excitement that I was trying something new; the fun was in the trying and in being with my family.

Dad continued to toss the balls. I hit myself with the racket more times than I hit the balls, and several times the racket flew out of my hand, which caused laughter from the gallery, my crazy, lovable family. I knew that they weren't laughing *at* me; they were laughing because the scene was indeed funny. In fact, I was laughing the hardest. I thought I was going to topple out of the chair, I was laughing so hard. I blamed my misses on Dad's bad bounces and his peewee tosses. Julee wanted to toss me a few, and hers were even worse, either too high or too low.

"Well, no wonder I can't hit the side of a barn; no one will give me a decent throw." At that, Mom, Dad, Steve, Doug, and Julee, each picked up a tennis ball and threw it at the wall. I screeched, dropped the racket, and ducked. But I was defenseless: Four of the balls hit me. I yelped, then moaned in faked injury.

Spring was not only tennis season, but also golf season. Golfing had always been a very important sport in our family. My Uncle Harley was a golf pro at a country club, and Steve had thoughts about perhaps following in his steps. I had taken golf lessons with Steve at the country club Dad belonged to, and often our whole family would go out to play nine holes. Uncle Harley even had some clubs cut down to Julee's size.

Mom and Dad in no way wanted me to feel excluded in what they decided to do as a family. Mom sometimes felt a twinge in her heart, knowing that I longed to be out there playing—tennis, golf, doing cheers. But my longing to feel a part of the family, to be included in their activities even with my restrictions, more than outweighed the longing to be participating instead of spectating. Mom and Dad wanted me to do as many things as possible; we didn't just sit and watch television. Aside from Christy coming over and often going places with us, it seemed as if most of my other friends didn't have too much time for me. I saw them at school when I went to my three afternoon classes. They pushed me from class to class, and I knew they still liked me, but I was different which did cause some awkwardness. Because I wasn't strong enough to sit up all day and my bladder was still so weak, I didn't go to school all day. So aside from the three-hour exposure to my eighth-grade peers, I didn't see many other people other than my family. This caused us to grow together and to depend more on one another.

"Okay, let's go. Tee-off time is ten o'clock. Jama, you're going with us and don't try to get out of it by saying that you'll be in the way. Everybody's going. Julee get your clubs." Dad pulled his golf bag from the back door entryway. "This day's too beautiful to stay inside. Come on, Barb, get Jama into some shorts."

School had been dismissed for the summer only a few days previously; Dad wasn't wasting any time. I wondered how *I* could go golfing with them, but I didn't dare protest when he was ordering everyone around. I waited until we were in the car and then asked him what he was going to do with me.

"I've got this sheet that I brought, and we're going to get a cart and tie you in the seat," he answered.

"Can I drive the cart?" Julee asked excitedly, knowing that we didn't often splurge and rent a cart.

"No, hon. I think I better. We don't want to lose our passenger on a bump. But you can sit on the back by the bags and ride along."

"Oh, goody." She was appeased.

"How about us getting another cart for me and Steve?" Doug piped up from the back seat.

"No, I think you guys can handle walking nine holes," Dad laughed.

Dad drove the cart slowly around from hole to hole; I was tied securely in the seat with the sheet around my waist, and with all the force I had I held onto the arm bar at the side of the seat. We laughed, and I teased the boys and Dad about their hooks and slices and Mom about her unconventional putting stance. Everyone teased Julee about her short little clubs, and Dad and Steve tried to coach her. She would hit only on every other hole because she couldn't hit the ball very far. This resulted in so many strokes that Dad put only her putting strokes down on the scorecard; she was getting fours and fives just like everybody else, and she was very proud of herself.

I did not want to be part of every activity that Dad suggested though. When he proposed the idea of taking me over to the Ball State pool to go swimming, I did not want to go. It wasn't that I feared the water because I had nearly drowned during the accident; it was that I was embarrassed about my looks, my physical appearance, even around Mom and Dad for some reason. Because of lack of use, my arms, especially the forearms, were extraordinarily thin; and because I had little control of my abdominal muscles, my stomach protruded more than I thought it should. My petite, ninety-eight-pound frame was out of proportion, and I didn't want to put on a swimming suit. Dad said "phooey," that I was being ridiculous, and that I *was* going. He lectured me on the therapeutic qualities of water. Certainly no one could accuse Dad of pampering me or giving in to me. He made me go, which was normal for Dad; he knew that being in the water would be very good for my muscles.

I fussed and pouted every time Dad said we were going; but after we got to the pool and were in the water, my attitude improved and I enjoyed the buoyancy the water gave me. My arms and legs could move much more freely. Dad held my hands in his and as he walked backward, I would walk after him, slowly lifting one leg at a time. Mom walked beside me praising God all the while. Because Dad was on the faculty, he had a key to the pool area, so we went at a time when we had the entire pool to ourselves. This relieved some of the anxiety I had about people seeing me in my bathing suit. Dad and I praised God too, as we all bounced and danced our way around the pool. I may have been walking in the water, but I *was* walking!

8

Summer of 1970

With the summer of 1970, came a swelling anticipation that the completion of my healing was very near, the culmination of the little victories into one big triumph. Our whole family had made reservations to attend the world conference of the Full Gospel Business Men's Fellowship International at the Hilton Hotel in Chicago. We thought that might be the time and place for my full restoration.

Mom and Dad were excited about the meetings we would be attending—well-known teachers of the Bible, dynamic speakers, special meetings for the youth. They knew with overwhelming certainty that God and the awesome power of His Spirit would be there. They had both been fasting, and were in high spirits, charged with the energy of the Spirit, waiting on the edge of a miracle, claiming great things.

We kids were excited too. It would be our second time in the big city, and we all remembered how much fun we had had the first time. But we were anticipating, along with Mom and Dad, not so much seeing the city as seeing what God was going to do for me.

Julee was excited and jabbered about what we could do together after I got out of the chair. Even though I was doing things with the family, I was tired of being weak, tired of the frustrations, and tired of just watching the summer activities that I had always enjoyed doing. I wanted to lie out in the sun and get a tan, dash across the street to play with Christy, and practice cheers for the tryouts in the fall. In my heart and mind questions spun. Was this to be God's perfect time? Would He fulfill His promise in complete restoration? Would this be my time for walking and leaping and praising God?

These questions were also in the minds of my family, but only with the family and with the Klems did we discuss the possibility of me being healed during the convention. Even then, Mom and Dad said, "in God's time"; and yet, within a mother or father's heart, the time is always NOW. They both spoke to me in positive confessions as we packed and prepared to go.

"I'm expecting great things for you and for all of us," Mom told me.

"Me too, Mom, me too." My words were a prayer.

I prayed on the way to Chicago that my heart would be calm and at peace. I prayed for the Lord to cast out fear and the satanic suggestion that I would not be completely healed that kept slithering into my mind. I prayed that I would always remember that Jesus Christ is Lord. My head leaned against the back of the car seat, and I watched the countryside roll past. I thought about the women's luncheon Mom and I were going to—Kathryn Kuhlman, whose healing ministry was known worldwide, was the speaker.

Steve and Doug took turns pushing me around the hotel as we explored the huge dining rooms, lobbies, and gift shops with Kathy and Johnny Klem. Julee was off on her own with a couple of little girls her age, but when she got stuck playing on the elevator, her activities were quickly curtailed by father. We kids had never been in such a fancy hotel; we knew it was ritzy because the Coke in the machines cost a quarter.

On the day of the luncheon, Mom pushed me to the doors of the banquet room so that we could be among the first women in, to secure a seat at a front table.

"We'll just wait here so I can get you as close as possible. I want you to be able to see her, and there'll be hundreds of ladies here," Mom said, glancing down at me, her hand resting on the back of the wheelchair.

"Sure, Mom," I responded. As I waited, more and more women began to cluster around us, many peering at me with eyes of sympathy and curiosity. I thought about the dynamic ministry of

Kathryn Kuhlman, her spiritual aura. I had only heard about her ministry, especially in the realm of healing. This could be the day; this could be the day when God would manifest His healing power in me, fulfilling the work which He had begun. But I knew the healing would be from Jesus, and not from Kathryn Kuhlman. One prayer became urgent: *Lord, don't let me look to the name of Kathryn Kuhlman, but to the name of Your Son; let me look into His face.*

Closing my eyes, I felt the warmth of many bodies pressed together. Women were crowding over me. Sitting down while they were standing, I breathed in stale air, thickened with the scents of dozens of perfumes. The noise was a constant mixture of chatter and laughter, a buzz of excitement. I would have had to shout for Mom to hear me, so I remained silent and watched the waists of the women.

I wanted this to be the time, the day I would leap to my feet, moving and breathing as a completely normal person. I knew I would never be the same as I had been, spiritually. And I didn't want to be the same as I had been, physically. I wanted to be better, stronger. *Keep your eyes on Him; keep your eyes on Him,* I told myself, *God has all power.* The test was in trusting that He had complete control of my life and would not abandon me or leave me comfortless. The power of all the Scriptures I knew began building up great defenses around my vulnerable soul, bolting out the fear and anxiety that would tear down and destroy my faith. In extreme devotion to my belief in the Scriptures, I cried, *Yes, yes, Lord, let it be now.* I cried the words over and over in my head to drown out the whisperings of *maybe not, maybe not. God won't deny me; He is God,* I affirmed to myself.

An amplified voice announced, "Ladies, please move slowly to the tables. Your banquet tickets will be picked up at the tables." Movement forward was like opening the gates of the Kentucky Derby. Pushing me in and around the tables, Mom repeated, "Excuse me, excuse me. I have a wheelchair here."

"Take it easy, Mom. You're making me nervous. We don't have to sit at the very front table; I can see from further back."

"No, they have special places for people in wheelchairs so they can sit as close as possible. Here we are. Excuse me, please," she repeated again after bumping into a lady. She parked me almost underneath the speaker's platform and sat down next to me.

During the meal, Mom and I talked about my accident, the walk of trust and faith, the rejoicing victories. The ladies nodded and smiled and gasped, "Praise the Lord," and "Hallelujah." Mom did most of the talking, since I felt uncomfortable being the only teenager at the table.

The meal ended, and an expectant hush stilled the voices in the huge dining hall. After her right-hand lady, Maggie, gave a brief introduction, Kathryn Kuhlman swept from her seat, across the platform to the center podium. All eyes were upon her; her movements were graceful and lithe and balletic. As she prayed, her body flowed and swayed like a slender willow in a gentle breeze; her long arms and hands gesticulating. Love: From her message all I remembered was love. Her words floated through the room like a song, borne on the melody of His love. Now I better understood what I had heard about her: She had a spiritual effulgence that drew people to God by a wooing love. She glowed in His bright Light.

I was caught up in her liveliness, her vitality, her dynamic faith. Her love message was not long. From the message, she glided into a sweet and delicate dialogue with the Father. Her voice was continually musical, drawing out the vowel *o* in the name *God*. "Isn't God wonderful?" she repeatedly asked.

And the Spirit in the room said, "Come." All over the dining hall, ladies pushed back their chairs and stood up, moving forward, forming prayer lines. Prayers and praises mingled and blended to form a fragrant perfume that rose in pleasure to the inner courts of God. Women were crying, touched by God. The Spirit had descended, anointing hearts, washing away sorrows and hurts, lifting heavy burdens, baptizing with the oil of gladness.

I was filled with a sense of awe; my faith was generated to a new degree of intensity by the words she had spoken. But I felt no change, no miraculous electrical power flow through my body; I prayed that I would. I looked over at Mom, and I knew that her prayer was an echo of mine. Her eyes were moist; she closed them. Quiet praises tumbled from her lips.

Squirming in the chair, I tried to ignore the pressure. It only increased. The urgency tightened around my stomach. "Mom," I leaned over and whispered to her. "I have to go to the restroom. I'm sorry. I can't help it. I don't think I can wait until the meeting is over." I didn't want to leave. I didn't want to think that I could be missing out on what God had for me.

"You're sure?" Disappointment was in her voice.

"Yes. Sorry." I muttered, not looking in her eyes.

She pushed me out through the throngs of women, around tables and chairs. All the time, Mom felt the women were looking at her, thinking, *Why don't you stay and get that little girl prayed for?* Mom wanted to shout, "She's got to go potty!" Quickly we exited into the immense foyer and to the women's room down the hall.

When we returned to the meeting, Miss Kuhlman was still ministering, and the room was now jammed with all the people who had not made reservations, but came only to hear Kathryn. Rather than excusing our way through the crowd up to the front again, Mom and I decided to stay near the back since the meeting was nearly over. Besides, Maggie and Miss Kuhlman had descended the steps of the platform and were drifting through the crowd, praying, touching bowed heads.

A young man had edged his way over to us, and, looking down at me, began telling us about having faith in God to believe in miracles, that healing was what God wanted to do for His children. He repeated, "Just stand up, just stand up, and God will give you strength and you will walk. Just get up; believe in Jesus. He can heal you." He was not being forcefully obnoxious, but he seemed to be reciting all the "healing clichés" that well-meaning Christians are sometimes prone to use. He only wanted to help; I knew this. But I also felt a defensiveness rise in me, because I *did* believe in Jesus and I *did* know God could heal me. As he talked about faith and healing and miracles, I lowered my head, the tears rolling down my cheeks. Mom was also crying, as our spirits petitioned God for this to be the time. We were both begging, pleading, claiming, promising—almost anything, if only God would touch me. Finally, the young man's continuous exhorting became too much; I'd had all the faith talk I could take. I looked up at him through my tears and very firmly and staunchly declared, "I'm already healed. I was healed the night that my mother and dad prayed for me." I did not want to be cruel or to crush his spirit, but I didn't want to hear words as much as I wanted to feel and see results.

Now I prayed that the healing I knew was mine would be manifested so that others would also know that I was healed. Straining my neck, I watched as Kathryn floated across the floor, coming farther back, her long gown rising and falling with each graceful step. She was coming closer. *Jesus, Jesus,* my soul whispered. I waited, sobs building, swelling from the deepest part of my heart, sobs of *Yes, Lord, please.*

Most of the women had risen to their feet; some reached out and touched her as she passed. She continued toward the back of the room. Mom pushed me closer into the aisle so that Kathryn would see me. As Mom lifted me up out of the wheelchair and onto my feet, we were both almost totally overcome with emotion, and we waited. Would God's power flow through my body, making it strong again?

In her white, flowing dress, Kathryn swept over the carpet toward us. As she passed by, I looked into her shining eyes, eyes that gleamed with His love. I smiled, saying nothing; she smiled back. "Touch her, Jesus," she spoke moving past me, her delicate fingers brushing across my arm. My legs became weak, and Mom, also weakened from supporting most of my body weight, set me back down in the wheelchair.

I had been waiting. Air was locked in my lungs. I had expected to feel something, some overwhelming sensation, some heat, some burning, some fire. I felt nothing. I sat still. I closed my eyes.

It was midafternoon but I felt like going to bed when Mom and I went back to the room after the luncheon. The disappointment lay like lead on my heart, and I knew Mom felt it too. I struggled to trust, but my mind wanted to understand. The Scripture flashed through my mind, "Trust in the Lord with all thine heart; and lean not unto thine own understanding" (Proverbs 3:5). But I thought, *O Lord, it's so hard to trust right now when I wanted to be healed so much.*

Mom was reassuring as she helped me change out of my dress. "I know how much you were expecting something to happen, Jama. I was too. We all were. But just because God didn't complete His work today doesn't mean that He's not going to. We've just got to wait some more on Him. Perhaps He's got some other way of healing you than through one particular person's ministry."

"I know. I know, Mom." But the tears fell anyway.

Mom bent over the wheelchair and awkwardly tried to hug me as closely as possible until my tears were spent. Gently she whispered, "Jesus, Jesus," knowing that we both needed supernatural comfort that only He could give. Mom held me, and Jesus held us both.

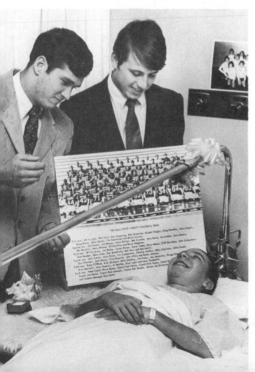

This is a yearbook picture of me when I was a seventh-grade cheerleader at Storer Junior High. It also hung on the wall while I was in the hospital. *Left:* Ball State football team co-captains Dwight Hodgin and Greg Shaeffer visited me in the hospital. They brought me an engraved pendant and an autographed picture of the team.

Thanksgiving 1970, one year after the accident. *Clockwise from left:* Julee, Steve, Doug, and me. *Below:* After being bald I never wanted to have my hair cut again. This is my high school senior picture (1974).

High school would have been lonely and less fun if Desiree hadn't been my best friend. *Below:* On my twenty-second birthday, our family went horseback riding in southern Indiana. I rode double with the guide; Doug is in the background.

Not all times in the apartment
were unhappy. Here, Joanne,
Mary, and I laugh at Chris as
she takes our picture. (Photo by
Chris Ann Stark.) *Right:* Chris
Stark, a dear friend and a wonderful photographer.

While I lived at home before John and I got married, we often played chess. I even won once! (Photo by Andy Oehler.) *Right:* This picture was taken just for fun during the summer. A month later it accompanied our engagement announcement in the newspaper. (Photo by Chris Ann Stark.)

John and I sent our wedding picture to friends and relatives as our Christmas cards in 1980. (Photo by Andy Oehler.) *Right:* As long as I am a part of the Ball State campus, I'll enjoy going to the Physical Therapy department in the Health Center. (Photo by Andy Oehler.)

Probably the one piece of equipment that makes me exert the most strength is the Universal weight machine. (Photo by Andy Oehler.) *Right:* At first I was terrified, but now I feel comfortable lecturing to and even joking with my classes. (Photo by Andy Oehler.)

One of the greatest rewards of teaching is seeing that flash of understanding cross a student's face. (Photo by Andy Oehler.) *Below:* This is our most recent family picture. *Clockwise from left:* Jama, John, Dad, Kathy (Steve's wife), Steve, Doug, Julee, and Mom. (Photo by Andy Oehler.)

9

The School of Trust

An unspoken disappointment traveled with our family when we left Chicago for home. Dad, the boys, and Julee, although they hadn't been in Kathryn's meeting, had expected to see me walking when Mom and I came back to the hotel room after the luncheon. But, as Steve said when we had been on the road for a while, "You know, we're disappointed, but this isn't the end."

And it wasn't. In diagnosing the meeting, trying to figure out God, our family came to the conclusion that God did touch me in some way. That became our pattern. Mom or Dad would encourage me, "Don't be totally discouraged; God did touch you in some way."

We all stood together united in the belief that I would be completedly healed; God was good to keep us from collapsing into utter despair because we didn't always *see* a miraculous change in my body. We felt that every time a person prayed for me I was touched. It could be spiritually or physically, but if a person prayed for me in faith for something to happen, then something did. This eased many situations for us: giving God credit for doing something in my life, rather than looking at my condition with our physical eyes and saying that, since we could see nothing, nothing happened. So many parts of my body needed help that many times we knew hidden parts were being touched when someone prayed.

Mom and Dad never wanted to deny anyone the marvelous beauty of praying for me. Yet, they did not encourage everyone who could pray to lay hands on me with the hope that *his* prayer would be the one that would cause me to leap from the wheelchair.

Now we all had to hold a little tighter to God's promises for healing. We had to believe just as Jesus healed in the Bible, so would He heal me. *Hold onto me, Lord,* I prayed, *because I am tired and weak.*

And hold me He did. He held onto me during those first anxious days of starting high school. Mom had arranged for me to have a key to the elevator, so I could get to my classes on the second floor; but, the lock was too high for me to reach from the wheelchair, and even if I could have reached, my hands were not strong enough to turn the large key. I had friends in every class, and they said that they would help me with the elevator when I had to use it. I was now strong enough to sit in the wheelchair all day, so I wanted to attend school for the entire day, not just the afternoon. Mom took me every morning, then came at noon to help me in the restroom, then returned after school to pick me up. This routine wasn't always easy or convenient for Mom, but she knew that it was a part of her life at the time and that I needed her. In her heart she knew that it would last for only a season. Her faith instructed her to look farther ahead to what she knew would come: my healing. Mom had to trust the Lord that my bladder would be strong. Dad knew her concern.

"You can't keep worrying about her day after day, honey." Dad's arms wrapped around Mom as they lay in the king-sized bed; her small frame was cradled by his side.

"But is she healed enough to go until noon when I go help her? Can she wait that long and then wait until the afternoon? You know that she can't get out of the wheelchair by herself."

"Yes, I know. But haven't we trusted God this far? Didn't we trust Him when we took out the catheter in the first place?" Dad tilted Mom's head and looked into her face. She knew he was right.

"But I just don't want her to have an accident and be embarrassed in front of her friends; she's already different enough."

"Honey, listen. He created her, He can fix her plumbing."

Mom giggled.

"So stop worrying, okay?" His faith pulled her up so that they were now standing on the same plateau in believing God.

And God did take care of my plumbing. Using the restroom in the nurse's clinic was the most convenient, because it had more room for the wheelchair than the narrow stalls of the girls' restrooms. Soon Mom and I became good friends with the nurse, Mrs. Haney. She offered to help me so that Mom wouldn't have to make so many trips back and forth. Abandoning modesty and embarrassment, I accepted, knowing that it would be easier on Mom. My friendship with Mrs. Haney grew during my high school years, to become something very special, even when I didn't require her help any longer. Mom and I called her an angel of mercy. We agreed that the Lord had a way of sending people at the right time to help me, and Mrs. Haney was certainly one of them.

My friends were very willing to push me wherever I had to go; I teased them that they were my "zippers" because they zipped me down the halls so fast. My wheelchair was sort of a novelty. Quite a few unsuspecting students walking to class in front of me had their heels clipped as I was zoomed to my classes. For some reason, every "pusher" wanted to see how fast the chair would go. We joked that maybe I should get a horn to warn others of my fast approach, or maybe I should go out for the track team.

My last class of the day during my freshman year was gym; in Indiana physical education was a requirement in order to graduate. I hurt inside at times, watching all the girls do the things I had loved doing. Gym class had always been my favorite. But then I was also glad that I could be there; my enjoyment became vicarious.

But I didn't always just sit and watch. Miss Michaels said that I had to earn my credit in more ways than just passing the written exams. She thought that I could hold the curved racket for the whiffle ball toss, which I could, but the trouble came when I tried to release the ball toward the person in front of me. Sometimes I'd throw the racket by mistake and then get teased that I was dangerous. Sometimes I'd release the ball, but it would fly directly above me because I didn't have the quick wrist action necessary to flip it forward. Then my partner would almost run into the wheelchair trying to catch the ball with her racket. I had to learn to laugh along with everyone else, knowing that the laughter wasn't directed at me or my condition or attempts, but at the results: the ball and the racket flying everywhere.

In faith, Mom bought new tennis shoes for me, believing that I would be able to wear them in gym class. But it takes more than tennis shoes to move God. Once more she learned that the healing isn't in what we do; it is in God's sovereignty and faithfulness.

One day when Mom came to the gym door after the last bell of the day had rung, I told her about the class.

"Mom, I was just sitting there watching the kickball game a few girls had started during free time, when someone came up from behind and raced me around the bases, screaming, 'Home run! Home run!' I thought I'd fall out of my chair I was laughing so hard! It was really funny! And then Ellen tried to play catch with me, but I couldn't throw the ball very well because, you know, my fingers. But I shoved it and it sort of rolled out of my arms. It bothered me that I couldn't throw it, but Ellen said she didn't mind, that at least she didn't have to run across the gym to get it, so that made me feel better. She bounced it into my lap, and sometimes, it would bounce up and hit my chin; then I'd roll it to her. We didn't play very long though because my arms got tired. But it was still fun." I rattled on and on as she pushed me down the hallway. "See you guys tomorrow!" I yelled to a group of friends coming out of the girls' locker room. They waved and yelled good-bye.

I hadn't noticed Mom's face when I was chatting about the gym activities because she was pushing me from behind, but she had cringed and cried inside for what I was yet unable to do. She knew how she and Dad had worked with my hands, how my fingers had been little fists and had to be pried open. My hands didn't look quite normal then, and she didn't want my friends to see my frailty and abnormality. She wanted the world to see me as a normal young girl who just wasn't walking right then. It became another instance where God almost had to shout to her, "Let go and let Me. I'll see her through."

My hands became stronger as I used them more. God gave me other muscles to use to accomplish what usually required minute finger usage. In Home Economics sewing class, I made Mom a pantsuit which she wore with great pride. In art class, I carved a dove in bas-relief on a flat piece of board; the wood was extremely hard, and I had to use gouging tools. Since my right hand was stronger, I used it, but I could still work only a short while at a time because my hand got tired. How I finished it I'll never know; I still have two scars on my fingers from the gouger slipping out of my right hand and cutting into my left. But Mom hung the completed dove on our kitchen wall and boasted of it to company.

The first time the gouger slipped and sliced into my index finger, Mom reacted as any mother would when she saw the blood-soaked bandages: She wanted to keep me from ever being hurt or injured. *If only that teacher would realize what an accomplishment it is for her just to hold the tool, maybe he'd give her easier projects,* she thought. She wanted me to be treated as any other student, asking no special favors. But when she saw me struggling to chip away the wood or carefully pull the needle and thread through the fabric as I hemmed, she wanted to change her mind and yell, "Treat her special!" When this happened, God's grace was faithful to remind her that He was working *in* me, that He wanted me to be a total person, and I couldn't be if I was pampered and babied.

The cut finger was a minor injury; I had had worse cuts and bruises before the accident that Mom hadn't worried too much about. Now she had to keep trusting God to watch out for me and to protect me when she wasn't there beside me. The dove became significant to Mom; and even now when she thinks of it, pride floods her soul: pride in me for seeing through a difficult task, and pride in Jesus for giving me the strength, determination, and grit to finish the task. And the dove reminded her how much she had to keep trusting Jesus.

Throughout the school year, God helped me and gradually infused me with more of His patience, more of His love, more of His healing. By the time summer came, I was in the wheelchair only when I was out of the house; in the house, I used the walker all the time. My steps had become quicker, my legs responding with hastier obedience to the signals from my brain: *Pick up, put down, pick up, put down, and quit shuffling your feet.* I had stopped going to the hospital for physical therapy, but Rudy, a trainer from the Ball State football team, began coming over to the house and helping me with exercises on the floor. He showed Dad and the boys different exercises to build up my arm and leg muscles. At times, I felt like a pretzel as they twisted me in many positions.

It was time for another step of faith. Along with the budding and evidence of rebirth seen in nature, I too had to blossom and demonstrate the evidence of my growth and progress. I had taken the step from the wheelchair to the walker; now it was time to put the walker aside and take a new step in faith. As a family we were united in the belief that God was continually working. We were not about to give up and accept that my recovery would be limited only to partial use of my limbs, that I had recuperated as far as was medically possible for an injury of my nature. Medically, I wasn't even supposed to recover as far as I had. No, we had set our goals high, high as the throne of God, and we knew that He wasn't finished yet.

"Jama, I was talking with Rudy the other day about how much stronger you're getting, and he suggested that we try out a pair of crutches," Dad said as we sat around the table after church one Sunday, eating dinner. "What do you think?"

I remembered the crutches I had used for three weeks when I had had my foot in a cast in the third grade. I had injured my ankle by accidentally sticking my foot in the spokes of a bicycle while riding double. I wasn't so sure that I could maneuver those kind of crutches that went under the arms. I voiced my doubt.

"No, they wouldn't be that kind, Jama. He called them elbow crutches. They're made of metal, and they have some kind of part that fits around the lower part of your arms. I'm not really sure what they look like, but I thought I'd go over to the place where we rented your wheelchair and see if they have any. We might as well give them a try, right?"

"I think it's a great idea." Mom agreed.

I'll be more than happy to get rid of that walker, I thought. "Yes, might as well," I said.

Dad brought home the crutches the next afternoon. Parked in

the living room, I felt emotions swirl within: a dry excitement, a thrill of succeeding, a dark shadow of fear that I wouldn't be able to perform up to my expectations, nameless flutters. Like a glory procession, Mom, Steve, Doug, and Julee marched in behind Dad. They stood around the room, waiting and praying, with eyes wide with love and hope, to see me do something I hadn't been able to do before.

"Here, Mom, you take these crutches, while I help her to her feet."

"No, Dad. Let me do it. I can get up by myself. If I'm going to learn to use those, then I'll have to be getting up out of chairs by myself." I didn't mean to talk with defiance, but I felt it scorch my voice. I saw hurt flash on Dad's face. "I'm sorry, Dad. Didn't mean to say it that way." My pride had stiffened; I didn't want any unnecessary help.

"Okay. Okay. That's all right, J. Just push yourself up and when you have your balance, I'll help you with the crutches and Mom can wheel the chair away."

I still had to concentrate and focus all my energy on pushing my body to a standing position. I swayed this way and that, like a rickety gate. Mom and Dad held their arms ready to catch me in case I lost my balance. I kept my hands within reach of the chair until I felt balanced enough to have Mom pull it away. No breath escaped until I was secure.

"Dad, you can hand me one of them now." He held one arm and helped me slide my other arm through the metal cylinder. Pushing the back of my hand against the hand grip caused my fingers to extend enough to grasp the handle—something I had learned while using the walker. My hands were still tight fists of contracted muscle.

"It feels awkward, Dad. I think it's too tight around my arm." He pulled the cylinder open further. With both of my arms in the crutches, I stood there. "Feels weird. Maybe they're not the right length."

"Just take a few steps, and then we'll be able to tell," Dad said. "I'll be right here. You won't fall."

"Jesus is right here, too, Jama. He won't let you fall," Mom declared, pulling the wheelchair away into the entry hall. "Start praying, Jama. And you kids, too. God's doing a new thing; He's taking us another step."

"Easy on the sermon, Mom," Dad teased her. We kids started laughing.

"Wow," I tottered, nearly losing my balance.

"I've got you." Dad put his hand against my back for support. "Barb, just stand on the other side of her while she's walking. Now, Jama, Rudy said to lift one crutch and one foot at the same time, left foot with right crutch, right foot with left crutch." He demonstrated with invisible crutches.

"Okay, I get it. I better try it before I'm worn out from standing here."

"Let's move it, J," Doug teased.

Slowly, I lifted the crutch, replacing it a few inches ahead of its original position. I picked up my right foot and took a baby step forward. I moved each foot and crutch one at a time, like a four-legged machine. The movements were stilted, labored.

"Well, it's not exactly like Rudy said to do," I said after I had moved halfway across the living room. Maybe it'll take some practice before I'm used to it, just like it did with the walker."

I was rationalizing my slowness, my awkwardness, but then I realized that I didn't have to. I looked at the faces of my family. Everyone was watching me with silent, happy grins. Their faces exalted God because I was out of the wheelchair on my feet, standing, walking. Their grins infected me. I saw the distance I had walked on the crutches. I felt my smile go deep, through my heart, my soul, my spirit, all the way down to my toes.

Dad put the wheelchair in the basement. Julee, the boys, and Christy were glad because they could have all the wheelchair races they wanted. All summer I practiced on those two crutches. The house pulsated with the vibrance of His Spirit and the hope of His promise. We praised God for the many "firsts" I was able to do: the first time I could stand at the sink and help load the dishwasher, which had been my old job before the accident; the first time I could completely dress myself, buttons, zippers, shoelaces;

the first time I could go to the restroom alone; the first time I could use scissors.

The fresh outpouring watered my heart again with God's love and goodness. During the dry spells when I could see no progress, when I would try to do something new and fail—like dropping a pencil on the floor and not being able to bend down far enough to reach it—I fought a tiring battle against discouragement and despair. As a headstrong teenager, I didn't want more virtuous patience as much as I wanted divine healing.

But the summer was a glad time: the sun, the freedom, no responsibilities, no studies. And for me, it was a glad time for walking. No more did the wheelchair have to be folded up and loaded in the car whenever I went anywhere. Now, being out of its confines, like a prisoner set free, I felt much more a part of my family, much more a normal youngster. A chair didn't have to be removed at the dinner table so I could be wheeled up. I sat in a kitchen chair just like the rest of the family. When I watched television, I sat on the couch or in any other chair I wanted. I fought again with the boys and Julee for the most comfortable chair. At church, I didn't have to worry about blocking the aisles with the wheelchair. I loved sitting in the pew with the rest of my family again.

At first, someone had to help me up from the chair and especially from the couch, because I was sitting much lower than I had been in the wheelchair and I couldn't seem to get the proper leverage. Learning how to manipulate the two crutches took some time. Once I was in the standing position, someone had to hand me the crutches.

One night when we were in the living room waiting for Mom to call us to dinner, I began planning a strategy. I looked at the crutches, the couch armrest, the height of the couch. I looked at my legs and knew they had the strength. *I can do it*, I thought.

"Time to eat," Mom's voice announced from the kitchen.

"Okay, kids, let's go." Dad started over to the couch to help me up.

"Race you guys," Julee shouted, dashing around the corner.

Steve and Doug took the quicker route through the dining room. I heard Julee squeal.

Dad was reaching down for the crutches lying on the floor. "Wait a minute, Dad," I said. "Let me get them. I want to try it by myself. I think I can get up."

"Sure." He grinned. "I think you can, too."

I gripped one crutch with my left hand and leaned the other against the couch so I could reach it easily when I stood up. Wiggling my body forward on the couch, I estimated at what point I would have the best leverage. The left crutch was at a forty-five-degree angle to the floor; my right hand was at a ninety-degree angle to the armrest. With a trumpet call to action, I pushed against the grip of the crutch and the armrest simultaneously. But halfway up action halted, and I fell back onto the couch. I sighed.

"No, Dad. Let me try again. I know I can do it," I vowed determinedly. Readjusting my grip on the crutch and putting it at a little lower angle, I clenched my jaws unconsciously. I was ready again. The trumpet sounded again and I pushed. A groan escaped. At the crucial halfway point, I inched the left crutch closer as a balance support.

I straightened all the way up and arched my back to relieve the tenseness of concentration. I stood there. Dad looked down at me and whispered, "Praise the Lord." My eyes raised into his; my heart and voice echoed his tribute.

"Yes, praise the Lord, for sure." I released a happy sigh and reached behind me for the other crutch. "Let's go eat, Dad. I'm starving." Together we walked slowly to the kitchen, my steps halting and abrupt, but steps of victory.

Being able to get out of chairs and off couches gave me a new sense of independence. But I still needed someone walking behind or beside me for security, because my balance was unsteady. Both hands were busy holding the crutches and if someone wasn't near when I wobbled, I would fall, since I didn't have a free hand to reach for a wall or a chair to steady myself. Venturing out solo in my walking was a matter of conquering a fear of falling. To be a conqueror, I had to rely on the power of the Lord and the presence of my guardian angel to be my steady arm. During my Bible reading, I found a new Scripture to stand on in Psalms 116:8,9: "For thou hast delivered my soul from death, mine eyes from tears, and my feet from falling. I will walk before the Lord in the land of the living."

I realized that if I ever wanted to make it on two crutches at school I had to overcome that overpowering fear. I had to trust God completely. Another Scripture brought comfort: ". . . I will never leave thee, nor forsake thee" (Hebrews 13:5).

Take me in Your arms, Lord, I prayed, *melt away my fear.*

Once I was walking on the crutches and getting up from a seated position, the next step was going up and down our stairs. I had moved back into my bedroom upstairs about six months after I came home from the hospital, but Dad had to carry me up the stairs every night and down every morning: no easy load. The stairs had a railing, which I held onto, and one step at a time, up and up I went. For me it was like mountain climbing.

The more I walked, the more confidence I had. As much as I wanted the security of someone's presence, I also wanted independence. *An independent person doesn't rely on others unnecessarily,* I told myself. I had to demonstrate and assert this independence by declining help, by telling Mom or Dad or anyone else, "No, you go on in the house. I can make it up these steps alone." The steps were the three outside our house—hard, cement steps. Going up was easier than coming down, but either way I prayed, *Lord, keep me balanced. Don't let me fall.*

But I wasn't always gung ho about doing all I should to increase my muscle strength and independence. Dad had purchased a stationary bicycle for me when Rudy had told him that biking was good overall body exercise. As with the swimming, Dad had to force me to ride that bike. It took two people to get me on the seat, and then, because my rear was sensitive, I complained that the seat was uncomfortable. At first my feet would constantly slide off the pedals, and I was unable to make one complete rotation. Rudy finally brought over some leather straps that Dad used to secure my feet onto the pedals, but still I resisted riding the bike. Dad would say yes; I would say no. He would win; I would cry. I felt uncomfortable and frustrated because I was so clumsy and awkward at trying to make the pedals work.

My rear gradually became less sensitive to the tiny seat, and I could make the pedals rotate easier, but whenever Dad said, "Bike time," I groaned. But I rode it and watched TV to keep from being bored and to make the minutes go faster.

With walking everywhere I went and the bicycle exercise, my endurance and mobility increased. Getting anywhere took time since my steps were still very slow; I was cautious and paused to rest if I had a long distance to walk. Every few yards I had to stop, rest, and regain my balance. I lacked momentum and consistency. At times I could walk faster than at other times. My family had to be patient with my walking, and we learned to make small talk about things we saw as we slowly walked along. The wheelchair had been easier in many ways in that they could dash with me to get out of the rain or to the nearest restroom.

Yet, as the summer progressed, I progressed. An urgency within signaled that I must practice hard at my walking to establish a stabler balance so I could walk at school. I didn't want to go back to the wheelchair again. I wanted to be as independent as I could.

During the hot, sultry days of August, a burning heat began to simmer within me. It was an oppressing heat, fiery, full of anxiety. Terror seized me with iron strength, threatening to suffocate my joy of improvement, to destroy my victory flag. I had to overcome a greater fear of beginning another year of school than I had had to when I entered high school in the wheelchair. I knew as long as I was in the wheelchair, I had no real physical demands; I had only to sit and be pushed. Now that I was walking, I had to rely on my own strength to get from one place to the other. I had to depend on myself instead of others. And this independence was something I wanted and yet didn't want. I didn't want it because it saddled me with too much responsibility. The doubts and questions flooded in.

Would I be strong enough to walk all around the school building every day? What if I fell? How would I carry my books? Could I walk fast enough to get from one class to the other in five minutes? These questions boomeranged in my mind even though I knew the answer to each one: Jesus. I knew I couldn't do it by depending on my own strength. Alone, I couldn't do anything.

I went to the Bible again, to Proverbs 3, "Trust in the Lord...." I went to Isaiah 40:29,31, "He giveth power to the faint; and to them that have no might he increaseth strength.... But they that wait upon the Lord shall renew their strength; they shall mount up with wings as eagles; they shall run, and not be weary; and they shall walk and not faint."

I was young emotionally, physically, mentally, and spiritually, but I was growing, maturing. And the progress of my healing was parallel to my spiritual progress. It was a step-by-step process. Sometimes both processes were so slow that frustration was overwhelming; sometimes they were so quick the transformation was unsettling. With each improvement, new things were required of me: When I could stand at the sink, I had to help with the dishes; when I could reach across the bed, I had to make it, no matter if it did take me longer.

Likewise, with each spiritual revelation or teaching, I had to apply the knowledge: When I learned that I had to act on my faith, I had to step out on the water; when I knew that God wants His children to "prosper and be in health," I had to believe that He would direct me into a career and give me divine health. I wouldn't go backward, either physically or spiritually. I would go forward, with boldness that would bulldoze through fears and embarrassments, through intimidations and frustrations. I wanted to blast through the darkness of fear and into the shining Light.

And I was learning how to do things for myself, how to have more patience, how to trust God to take care of what I couldn't do yet. I gave Him my sophomore year. I gave him the anxiety and the fear. I gave Him the loneliness and the desire for friends. I gave Him the pressures and the awkwardness of my walking. I gave Him my tears and my dreams.

I gave Him myself, my faith, and my trust.

10

One Down, One to Go

When I gave God my sophomore year, He gave it back to me pressed down and overflowing. He knew my need for companionship and gave me Desiree, a girl I had known for a few years but who had just become a Christian in early September. When Desiree became a Christian, not only was her life changed, so was mine. Our friendship grew, dissolving the loneliness I had felt during my freshman year.

It wasn't as though I was friendless. I had friends and was never neglected during school hours. But other than Christy, I had very little companionship after school and during weekends. Christy and I were now in different schools, and I realized the gap of our two-year difference. I needed friendship and companionship outside of school. No one could take Christy's place in my heart, but I felt the need for more than one close friend. Depending on Christy for all my companionship needs was unhealthy for both of us. Desiree became more than another companion: She became my friend.

Not only did God give me Desiree, He also gave me a Christian youth group for fellowship. During my sophomore year, God was moving in the lives of many young people, in my high school and in other schools around Muncie. The youth population at our church increased, and Mom and Dad felt that they should start having youth meetings at our house again. Ted Evans, the new youth minister at our church, was also excited about starting a fellowship. So the Friday night meetings at the Kehoe's began again. Jesus was stabilizing many new friendships that were causing us to know Him better.

My sophomore year was not as fearful as I had thought, and the Lord faithfully answered all of those tormenting questions. My strength increased day by day as I walked through the halls, and the teachers didn't mind my being late to their classes. They were thrilled to see me walking. I had friends in each class who would carry my books to my next class and help me with the elevator when I needed it.

God took the doubts and gave me confidence. He took the awkwardness and gave me more mobility, more finger dexterity. I continued my Home Economics sewing and cooking classes and my art classes. I became comfortable in my progress. I wasn't ready for a change as sudden as the one God wanted to give me.

Summers seemed to be my time for stepping out on the waters of faith and trust. It was June 1972. I was at a Full Gospel Business Men's Fellowship meeting when I heard the crash. Opening my eyes, I looked slightly over my shoulder to the wall where I had leaned my two crutches. They weren't there. I thought that they had caused the crash. They were always falling and getting knocked around. I didn't think anything more about them, but closed my eyes again as we ended the meeting in prayer. We were standing in a circle, holding hands. My stance had become straighter, my body stronger. When standing, I would only sway if I kept my eyes closed for a long time.

The prayers slowly silenced. Around the room, eyelids were opening; eyes were aglow, lights of God. As people began hugging and shaking hands, Mom went back to get the crutches. I sat down in the nearest empty seat. She returned carrying only one.

"They fell."

"I know. I heard them."

"But the other one broke. One of the screws must have gotten knocked out, because the whole top of the crutch is off. I looked for the screw, but couldn't find it anywhere."

"Well, Mom, could you look again? I need to go to the restroom."

She looked again, but still no screw. The crutch lay in two pieces on the floor, useless. Mom gave me the one crutch. "I'll help you. Here put your hand in my elbow."

An irritation erupted. Where was my faith? I wondered as I walked beside Mom. I chastened myself: *Here I am in a room with strong, believing Christians who are dedicated to walking the Spirit-filled life, and I am so self-conscious and preoccupied with not being able to use the two crutches that I'm letting all the joy and peace I just experienced in the meeting slip away.* My eyes of faith were closed as I viewed my situation. My eyes were closed. All I could foresee were problems, even disaster, if I had to rely on only one crutch.

Coming back to the table where Desiree was, with Mom still at my side, I kept my eyes on the placing of the crutch, carefully avoiding water spills, any slippery spots. I finally glanced up and saw Desiree's eyes glistening when I approached her. She saw that I was using only one crutch; the corners of her mouth turned up in a slow gentle smile. I looked away, not being able to understand what was happening in my mind, my spirit, my soul. A boiling storm of fear darkened inside, and yet quiet breezes were stilling that fear, calming the great surges of resistance and anxiety. I knew I had to give this next step into the Father's care once again. I had to release willingly that to which I was clinging.

Some of the people who were still in the room noticed that I was using the single crutch. Their expressions were bright, "Glory." I wished that I felt their anticipation; apprehension gnawed inside me. But outside, I was smiling. "Yes, the Lord, is truly wonderful," I said, agreeing with them, and meaning it sincerely. I knew He was wonderful, I just couldn't understand the way He worked sometimes. The same questions I struggled not to think about surfaced: *But if God is so wonderful, why doesn't He complete my healing right now? Boom, totally, instantly, no waiting. Why do I have to go through with more patience building? Haven't I learned enough in these last three years?*

My spirit was fighting to suppress the storming questions, to cling to my peace which passeth understanding, to my confidence, while my flesh was pulling and warring, a declaration of mutiny and rebellion.

"It looks like you won't be using this one for a while. In fact, I'm believing that you won't be using it again," Mom said, laying the broken crutch across the table. She was always stepping out in boldness and unshakable firmness in her confessions. For her, if you believe it and you say it, it happens. Sometimes her attitude frustrated me because I felt that she didn't know how hard it was for me to keep taking faith steps; after all, she could just get up and walk around without any difficulty. I *did* believe. I believed so hard that I thought my chest might split open and my heart pop out, but I was tired of the progress being so slow, so challenging. Over and over, I said, *Lord, I'm healed; I know that You've healed me.*

Dad came across the room, saw the broken crutch, looked at me, and smiled. "So, it's down to one, huh?" He kept grinning.

I smiled weakly. "Yes, I guess so."

I didn't remember that I had fought the same battle against change once before when I had stepped away from the wheelchair and the walker to the crutches.

Trying not to let fear show on my face—the fear of falling, the fear of failing, the fear of being unable to walk with a single crutch —I kept the smile plastered to my face.

"One down, one to go, right? He'll do it. I just wish He'd do it a little quicker," I chuckled; inside, I was serious.

"Then you think we ought to just leave the broken crutch here?" Dad asked.

I hadn't thought about the fact that the crutch *could* be fixed. The voice of the Spirit was clear. I listened.

"Yes. Let's leave it," I said, while thinking, *Lord, don't renege on me, on my step of faith.*

"Well, Jama, it's been a slow healing so far. Let's praise Him for another step. He's working. We'll go step by step together." Dad took my arm, crooked it into his elbow and escorted me to the door.

The storm passed, and I felt safe. It would be all right; I had the strength and faith of my family and friends to support me when I wavered. I didn't have to walk alone. God loved me; He wouldn't take away any support until the proper time, when I would be strong enough to walk alone. I guess He knew I was ready for the next step. Claiming His promise again, "I will never leave you, nor forsake you," I watched my feet as I walked slowly, very slowly, beside Dad. The words were comfort; I knew His presence.

I kept stepping forth through the summer, but not always freely and not always joyfully. Walking with the two crutches, I had a measured portion of independence and confidence when walking by myself. If I didn't have to worry about a purse or books, I could manage alone. Security was in two crutches. Now security was broken; walls of dependency closed in on me again, stifling and threatening. With one crutch, my balance was shaky; I had minimal confidence in my walking stability. Because I had to concentrate on keeping my balance with every step, my feet moved in inchworm steps; it took me longer to get from one place to another.

My insecurity made me want to get the other crutch fixed; I was comfortable with two, because there was less struggling. But that would be going backward, giving up, a denial of what God was doing, of His power. Attacks of pity and frustration weakened my vulnerable spirit. By going back, I would be taking the easy way out, the way that was most comfortable. From the beginning of the accident, my healing had not come easy; I realized that it probably was not going to start now. My strength was in short supply; I knew that I had to rely on His power, His security. My family knew my fears and frustrations, especially Mom and Dad, but rarely did I ever mention them to anyone else, probably for fear that my faith would seem weak and my doubts unchristian.

By surrendering the one crutch, I had surrendered part of my independence. Again, I needed someone near while I walked, in case I might fall. Again, my family was there, uncomplaining and patient. I had difficulty becoming accustomed to one crutch; I depended on an arm or a hand as a substitute crutch. Because of this insecurity and fear of losing my balance, I would take shortcuts when nobody was near to walk with me. I patterned the easiest way, the way that would give me something to balance against as I went by—walls, tables, doors, anything I could touch. Anything that was strong and stable became my second crutch.

My fear was blinding me from stepping out in complete faith.

I could improve only to the degree that I was willing to surrender totally to God, allowing Him to work out my healing in His divine way. And improvement meant change: I had to accept using one crutch and learn to concentrate fully on walking as a praise offering to God.

Remembering how I had forced myself to practice walking with the two crutches, I practiced walking with one. Just as with anything I had tried before—studying, cheerleading, gymnastics—I had to work at walking. Unless there is a chance of success, no one will try anything. I wanted success, so I practiced my walking. But at times with gritted teeth.

The youth camping retreat planned for July provided me with an incentive for straighter, more confident walking on my part. I wanted to go down Friday morning with the group that was setting up the tent, rather than late Friday night with my parents and Julee. And I wanted to be walking with balance secure enough that I wouldn't have to ask anyone to help me. The desire to be as normal and as active a teenager as possible was intense. Steve would be going down early too, but I didn't want him to feel he had to be with me every second. He and Desiree had begun dating, and I didn't want to be a third wheel. We three enjoyed each other, but I knew that I had to give Steve space to enjoy his time alone with Desiree.

As soon as I made the decision to go with the morning group, the tug-of-war began. Negative questions pulled: *What if you have to go to the bathroom? Mom won't be there to help you. Will they have restrooms close to the camping site? You'll be in trouble if you have to walk far. What if you have to go up steps? You'll have to ask someone to be the "railing."* What if? What if? But the positive answers were stronger, pulling me away from pride and possible embarrassment. These people were friends, and, more importantly, they were Christians, brothers and sisters in the Lord. I determined that nothing would stop me from having a good time, fellowshipping with friends, rededicating myself to the Lord.

"I'll watch you guys set up the tent from here," I said. Steve parked the station wagon close to the grassy campsite. I opened the car door and swung out my tanned legs.

"You've got the easy job. Do you know how hot it is already? Just look at the size of that tent, too. It's a *circus* tent," Steve exclaimed and teased. "I hope we don't pass out before we get it up!"

"Oh, you can handle it. Look at those muscles bulge!"

"Oh, yes!" Steve agreed as he flexed a bicep. Desiree and I laughed. Then he dashed over to help the other guys already unwrapping the huge tent.

Even with the door open, the car was stifling. I had noticed almost immediately when we pulled up that outhouses were situated about a hundred yards beyond the campsite. "Praise the Lord," I whispered. In front of the tentsite I noticed a picnic table. My mind surveyed, calculated, estimated the distance, the bumpy weeded ground, the lack of supports, trees, tables. Ironically, the song about "keeping your feet on solid ground" popped into my head. *You can do it,* I coached myself.

Leaning the crutch against the side of the car, I pushed up from the seat and reached for the open door to steady my balance. If I didn't move fast, I knew that fear would leaden my body to that car seat until someone came to walk beside me. A deep breath was the starting gun. Tiny steps moved me across the green—crutch forward, right foot forward, left foot forward, perspiration, prayers. Glancing up, I saw I had traveled half the distance. To me, it was halfway around the world. I watched my sandals sink into the warm grass with each step. My world had no noises, no shouts as the tent went up, no campers, no flies buzzing, only prayers to make it to that picnic table.

"Coming to help?" Steve's voice broke into my concentration. I jerked and nearly lost my balance. "Whoa!" He reached for me, but I caught balance and steadied.

I sighed in relief. "I'm okay."

"Here, allow me." He bowed like a gentleman escorting a lady and walked me to the table. His eyes had a mature tenderness, a love beyond brotherly affection. It was God's love.

"Thank you, kind sir." I winked.

The weekend was unforgettable. Scales dropped from my eyes. I saw that these friends looked beyond the crutch, beyond the slowness, to *me,* the me inside who wasn't crippled, wasn't slow. They saw in me the Christ who is whole. They looked at me with love. And love was the theme of the weekend. Love *was* the weekend: loving laughter, loving prayers. God knitted us into a garment of love. The love covered the embarrassment I thought I would feel about having Mom help me up from the low cot or to the outhouse. There was no staring, no questioning. They knew where I had been; they knew where I was going. So did I. The weekend was the Ananias hand touching Saul's eyes, touching my eyes.

When we returned from the weekend, the glory remained. I enthusiastically studied my Bible with a fervor I had never before experienced. It was the food and water for my hungering, thirsting soul. Rather than lie in the sun, I wanted to read the Word. "So then faith cometh by hearing, and hearing by the word of God" (Romans 10:17). My faith roots went deeper into the soil of Him. Because I knew with fuller knowledge to whom I belonged, I set aside demands for answers and reasons for my accident. I laid the "why" on the altar. I was tired of fighting. I yielded to Him. Answers weren't necessary; only He was necessary. He baptized me in joy.

The camping retreat was a turning point concerning my insecurity about social acceptance. I had felt accepted and loved for the person that I was, even if I was different. Except for being with my family, I hadn't felt that acceptance since before the accident. With these friends I felt included. But once school began, even though I had gained more mobility and greater independence on the one crutch, inferiority gnawed at the foundations of my friendships. I was different, and my awareness of the difference was a weight that lowered my self-image.

However, it was mostly through Desiree's love that I saw that my friends, my Christian friends, didn't see me as "handicapped" in the sense that the rest of the world did. Yes, I had my physical weaknesses, but didn't everybody have some weaknesses? Some just weren't visible to the physical eye. But when my difference gnawed with biting pain, I was still hesitant to accept an invitation to go any place because I walked so slowly.

With Christy I felt comfortable, because she understood my condition; I knew her motives for asking me to go to a movie or to a ballgame were pure. She asked in friendship, not in pity. I didn't want to be asked to do something out of pity—because "poor Jama would feel left out"—or out of guilt that they were having fun and I was sitting at home. I wanted to be asked because I was *me,* someone who was fun to be with—differences ignored.

My mind whirled with wanting to be involved in the teenage activities of my friends and with knowing that my slowness would make everyone wait. *For their sakes, I should refuse their invitations,* I told myself. Too many special allowances would have to be made: parking near entrances, or letting me out, so I wouldn't have so far to walk, giving me a hand or elbow when steps had no railing, holding packages when I went shopping.

"Yes, you are going," Desiree demanded one day after the school dismissal bell rang. "And I don't want to hear another word." We gathered up our notebooks and purses. The football game was at home that night.

I opened my mouth to protest. "But wouldn't you rather go with . . ."

"No," she cut me off. "I want to go with you, and I wouldn't have asked you if I didn't want to go with you. Now that's the end of it. Come on, I'll put my books in my locker and meet you at yours."

She went down one staircase to her locker. Now that I walked with the one crutch, I was able to use the stairs and had abandoned the elevator. I went down another staircase slowly, one step at a time. I had just arrived at my locker when I heard Desiree's wooden heels echo through the quiet halls.

"I'll pull the car up from the other lot and meet you outside." Lately, she had been driving her parents' car to school and had offered me rides home.

I was still walking down the sidewalk when she drove up. Patiently, she waited while I put my hand on the right fender of a parked car, stepped from the sidewalk into the parking lot, and slowly walked between the parked cars to her car. Sometimes I couldn't believe that Desiree was such a good friend to me. My fragile psyche longed to be loved and needed. I needed Desiree for a friend; I needed her companionship; I needed her laughter and smile.

That worry of being less needed began to fade as our growing friendship stabilized. She knew my temporary restrictions, and she assured me that I had much to offer, that I was special in her eyes. With a cord of love, she gently drew me from the loneliness of difference and social insecurity. Her love was from God.

I went to the football game that night with Desiree and to almost all the games that season of our junior year. Being with Desiree gave me a confidence in myself that I hadn't had since the accident.

Suddenly, the year was full of activity: I went with the family to watch Doug, who was now a freshman, play football and basketball; Desiree and I went to watch Steve wrestle; I went with Christy's folks to watch her play volleyball and basketball, and compete in track. I accepted more and more invitations to do things with others. With Desiree's encouragement, I was even bold enough to ask a guy from the youth group to the Sadie Hawkins Dance. We doubled with Desiree and Steve, and not being able to dance didn't matter since lots of kids went just to talk and watch and joke around. It was one of my few high school dates.

The youth group activities and all the boys' sporting events kept me so busy that I didn't dwell on the fact that I wasn't dating like other high school girls. With my increased mobility and strength, I was also less and less the focal point of our home. I didn't need someone to walk beside me all the time anymore.

During football season, all family attention was centered on Doug as we trouped to his games no matter what the weather. Then, during wrestling season, Steve received the glory, especially since he was in his senior year. I went to every match and tournament, swelling with pride in his ability and his victories. Our whole family was thrilled when Steve qualified for the state tournament, knowing that he was one of the eight best wrestlers in Indiana.

Julee was always a delight, and now that she was maturing into a very popular and independent sixth-grader, our childish quarrels were fewer: She became a wonderful combination of sister and friend.

As my self-sufficiency in taking care of my personal needs increased and my dependency on Mom decreased, I was able to stay overnight with Christy or Desiree. I didn't have to worry that I wouldn't be able to get out of bed alone or wouldn't be able to dress myself. Physically and emotionally I was getting stronger. However, I still required transportation to and from wherever I was going. Mom, Dad, Steve, or Desiree took me and picked me up without complaining or thinking of themselves.

The times when I was less self-sufficient were usually during the winters when the snow and ice came; then, just getting to and from the car was often treacherous. One snowy, slick morning when Mom took Doug and me to school (Steve had a study period the first hour and didn't come to school until later), fifteen-year-old Doug spoke words of wisdom to Mom and me, letting us know that the winter weather shouldn't restrict me from continuing to step forth in progress and independence.

"I sure wish that it would quit snowing," I said as Mom pulled up to the back door of Northside. She put the car in park, and I opened the door.

"Doug, here's Jama's purse; take it for her so she can concentrate on her walking in this snow and ice. And please let her hold onto your arm while she's walking to the door. It's really slippery, and she might fall." Mom handed Doug my purse which held my spiral notebooks for my classes.

"I'll take her purse in, but I won't walk with her, Mom. She's got to learn to walk in the snow and ice just like everyone else. You really pamper her sometimes, Mom. Instead of parking and driving her to the closest door so she won't have so far too walk, you should park the farthest away. You're not giving her a chance to walk; she needs the exercise. You're making it too easy. I'll watch from the inside to make sure that she's okay." His words were not spoken in cruelty, but in honesty, in faith that I could do more than I was doing.

Mom stumbled on her words, "But Doug, I've got my robe on

under my coat, I can't get out and help her. . . ." She looked from the icy, snow-covered sidewalk to me. I had swung my legs out the door and was getting ready to stand up.

"He's right, Mom. I'll be okay. I'll stick the crutch in the snow, away from the ice on the sidewalk, and I'll have more traction."

"Okay." Her voice was weak. "I'll pick you up here after school," she added as Doug shut the door behind me. I knew that she was praying fiercely for me and my stability as I walked up the sidewalk to the building. I heard the car motor idling as I walked, and she didn't drive away until I turned and waved my arm to her from the doorway.

God was continuing to make us stronger: stronger in faith, stronger in confidence, stronger in trust.

11

Senior Hopes and Fears

Because of my strength and increased mobility, I enjoyed school more and more. My junior year had been active and fun because I was involved in all the youth group activities and supporting the high school's athletic teams. I looked forward to summer as a break from studying, but I did miss seeing all my friends at school.

The summer was warm and relaxing, and I was quite lazy, spending many days just lying in the sun to tan. The three months went quickly, and I was glad to be back in school, knowing that I was finally a senior, one of the elite. Yet, I was also apprehensive because this was the beginning of an end—the end of high school.

But as I once again became the busy student, the thought of May graduation was buried under more pressing matters: going to Saturday night's football game, meeting my deadlines as a staff member on the yearbook, remembering the National Honor Society meeting on Tuesday, and of course, studying. It wasn't until December that I truly realized high school wasn't going to last forever.

"I'll let you out here and then meet you inside." Desiree pulled up along the curb. I leaned the crutch against the car door and pushed myself up. The December wind blew cold at me.

"It's freezing!" I shivered.

"Yes, I know! Shut the door!"

Laughing, I swung the door shut. Walking by myself up to the high school building, the cold fact that I was almost through with high school was as cold as the winter wind. Desiree and I had come to school at eight o'clock on a Saturday morning to take the Scholastic Aptitude Test needed to apply to college. I had taken the SAT as a junior, but the reality of college was distant then.

Now when I looked around the corner of my comfortable little world, college was a tidal wave coming closer to destroy my comfort. I didn't want to leave high school. I had been successful at avoiding the thought of the future and of the important decisions I would have to make soon, but this test was a reminder.

Future concerns remained dormant no longer. Through the Christmas holiday and into January 1974, when people saw me they would ask, "So you're graduating this year? What happens then? Are you going to college? Are you going to Ball State?"

Their questions were echoes of my own, and echoes have no answers. Although I was involved in more school and social activities, I still struggled with the idea of being able to manage in a college, going from building to building, carrying my own books, meeting new people.

Inside I wanted to continue my education; I liked going to school, studying, reading, learning. I felt satisfaction in making good grades. Because of my drive to excel scholastically, I was one of the top 15 students in my class of 325. I knew I could succeed in college intellectually, but I wasn't so sure about physically or socially.

To combat this uncertainty, I worked at erecting a citadel; the erection was not elaborate, but it was deliberate. I told myself that soon I would be totally healed and then I wouldn't have any problems deciding what to do. I'd be able to go to college along with all my friends. I was looking for the complete manifestion of my healing as the answer to all the questions. And I was looking at the January meeting of the Full Gospel Business Men's Fellowship as the date for that manifestation. Jimmy Clark, a friend of our family's for many years and a dynamic black preacher, was the speaker. Because God had blessed him with a powerful ministry, especially in divine healing, I felt certain that God would pour out His Spirit through Jimmy to me in that meeting.

One day, the week before the meeting, Mom picked me up from school, and I talked to her about my anticipation as we drove home.

"God's going to do something very special for me this Saturday,

Mom," I said, believing with my whole heart that He would. "Just think how it will be when this healing He started is finished." Her face smiled, her eyes smiled, her heart smiled.

"Yes, Jama. I'm believing with you." She nodded her head.

"And Mom, you know what?"

"What?" She glanced across the seat at me.

"Guess what I want for my birthday?"

"Your birthday? But that's not until April."

"I know, but guess what I want anyway."

"I don't know. What?"

I spoke in a positive confession, not wanting to give the devil a chance to rob me by speaking negatively. I spoke as if my healing was already done. "I want a new tennis racket. I think by then I'll be ready to take you on again on the court."

She laughed. "That's a deal. I think I can afford a new racket for you."

Time moved toward Saturday night. Expectation had my heart and mind on tiptoe. The healing was pictured in my mind: I could see Jimmy laying his hands on my head, as I had seen him do with others. The power of God would then flow through my entire body, recreating and restoring every injured part of the spinal cord, every muscle, every nerve.

It's going to be glorious, I thought. *I'll be able to praise the Lord in ways I long to, clapping my hands, raising my arms, dancing. God will do what He promised. This Saturday, He'll do it.*

Saturday finally arrived. As I sat in the back seat while Dad drove to the meeting, my concentration was a straight line: How great life would be after God healed me. My anxieties would be solved about going to college, about my lack of dating, about being physically different. I would be the person God had meant me to be.

I heard Jimmy preaching, but the words did not register. I was thinking too much about what would happen after he had finished.

Finally, he delivered an invitation for those wishing prayer to come forward. Men and women pushed back their chairs and moved to the front. The merging of prayer and praise and tears filled the room.

The front was crowded with people. I stood and waited. I couldn't move forward without bumping into someone. My eyes closed in prayer, a petition for God's anointing to fall on me. A gentle spring of tears trickled. I breathed with intensity, with fervency: "God touch me, touch me; I'm ready. Heal me with Your almighty power. Father, Father," I whispered.

When I opened my eyes, the crowd had thinned in front. Jimmy's eyes baptized me in love, and I saw him take a few steps toward me. I was standing near the platform, one hand resting on the back of a chair for balance, the other hanging by my side. I had left the crutch under the table. I took a step to meet him, but kept my hand on the chair.

A crescendo of prayer and praise lifted me up when people saw Jimmy place his hands on my forehead. My expectation for fire, electricity, the snap or pop of restoration was titanic, larger than any expectation I had ever had when someone had laid hands on me and prayed. The pressure of his hand warmed my head, but no fire raged, no sound exploded. Every energy cell in my mind and heart concentrated on God's healing me. I wanted it to happen now, instantly.

No thunder crashed from the sky; no drums rolled; no angels made declarations. When he removed his hand and his prayer silenced, I felt no different. *Feet, move,* I told myself. *Hands, move.* I pleaded for the freedom of my body, but the stillness remained. Jimmy took my hands in his own and walked backward. I followed him with slow, wooden steps. The sounds of prayer and praise grew louder, and I could hear Mom and Dad. I was walking alone without a crutch, but my body didn't have the loose flexibility and balance of a normal body. From the mountaintop of expectancy and awaiting, I fell to the valley of questioning and disappointment. Jimmy led me to a chair, and I sat down.

Attempting to veer my attention to the blessings of the Spirit, which had poured out over several lives during the meeting, was futile. All attention came speeding back toward me. My disappointment grabbed the "why" I had laid on the altar. *Why, God? Why didn't You heal me?*

In faith we had left the crutch in the banquet room of the

Holiday Inn where the meeting was being held, just as we had left the first crutch that had broken. But when we got home, I could no longer hold in the tears. I slumped onto the couch after Dad had walked with me into the house.

"Why? Daddy, why? Why didn't God heal my all the way?" I cried, the tears streaming down my face.

He held me tightly. Mom came and sat beside me on the other side, and we all held each other and cried. Mom's heart ached, and her throat was so tight she didn't think she could breathe. She had fasted and sought God diligently before the meeting, but seemingly our step in faith had produced very little. Mom hadn't cried with such hurt for me since the Kathryn Kuhlman meeting.

"Daddy, what did we do wrong? I can't go to school walking as I do now. I can barely take five steps. I still need the crutch." My voice cracked with hurt, and Dad brushed the tears from my cheeks and kissed my forehead.

"Honey, I have the same questions. I can't understand how I can hurt and be disappointed inside and yet have that peace that God is God, and He loves you beyond any love your mother or I could have for you. And in His love He has a plan for you that I guess we can't fully understand now. I know how you feel. Why shouldn't tonight have been the night for you to be walking and leaping about? I guess it's His timing that we don't understand. All the things that we've learned and been taught seem far away right now, but it's still clear that God is God. There is no ABC to healing. God has brought us back to the beginning—trusting Him. I know you want to question; I do too. But it's the trusting that's important right now, not the questioning. God's Word is still true, Jama." The Spirit of comfort and love were in his words and in Mom's hug.

"I just wanted it so badly. I'm so tired of being like this." The tears, which had stopped while Dad talked, began again.

"I know, sweetheart. I know," he whispered in my ear as his arms wrapped around me. I was encased by my parents, Mom on one side, Dad on the other, as they ministered to their hurting child.

I felt comfort in their arms and was soothed. My tears dried, and Mom helped me up to bed, taking the place of the crutch I didn't have.

"We love you, Jama," Mom said as she kissed me good-night. No other words were as important to me right then.

As I stared upward into the darkness, the comfort evaporated; I tried to make contact with God and regain the joy I had lost. I knew God loved me, as Dad had said. I knew it for a fact. *God loved me.* And His love was boundless and undying and pure. But if God loved me so much, why didn't He answer my prayer and heal me? Why didn't I receive something when Jimmy placed his hand on me and prayed? I cried and buried my face in the pillow.

"Lord, show me, please, why You are having me wait longer until You complete Your work in me. I need to know. I can't take this struggle with disappointment any more. I pray and expect and get excited waiting for You to do something, and then nothing dramatic happens. Show me, please." As I pleaded and wept, I fell asleep without seeing an opening in the dark cloud.

A few day later as I was sitting in the family room, Dad looked over at me from his recliner.

"Jama, I've got an idea. Let me walk with you like Jimmy did, letting your hands rest in the palms of mine. We have to trust and keep stepping out. Remember, the more you walk, the more God walks through you, making you stronger."

Dad stood in front of Mom's chair where I was sitting. He had gone back to the Holiday Inn to get the crutch we had left behind. He knew my heart still hurt, but he realized that we couldn't just sit and live on what God had done for me already. I wanted to be able to walk, but I didn't want to practice. I looked up at Dad and he just stood there. Relenting, I pushed myself up. I lost my balance and fell back into the chair.

"Oh, rats," I muttered. My heart was low on praise. I pouted, which siphoned out even more victory.

"One more time, Jama."

I was silent and pushed myself up again. My balance steadied. I walked with my clenched hands lying on Dad's open palms. Circling the family room, we headed back to Mom's chair. I knew I should have been rejoicing: I was putting one foot in front of the other, using no crutch for support. Here was the girl doctors had diagnosed a quadriplegic—walking! But instead of rejoicing, I prayed, pleading God to do even more to my body, to restore it completely.

Jesus, Jesus, help me, I love You, I need You. I can't do this alone. I am walking, but don't stop with this. Let me run. The words rushed through my mind.

"We'll go again at the next commercial," Dad said, holding my arm as I swiveled my body around and landed in the chair. Dad sat back down and picked up the newspaper. Staring beyond the television, I realized how ungrateful I was being. I repented and sacrificed my selfish hurt to receive again His joy, *I praise You, Lord.* I was in the dry wilderness searching for some answers.

In His mercy, He led me to a gentle stream of understanding. The entire week before Jimmy's meeting I had been praying and believing, I had been looking for an end result: my total healing. I had not been looking into the face of Jesus the Healer, the One who did the healing. My eyes were on the miracle, not on the Miracle-Worker. I was looking at the manifestation of my healing as the answer to all my problems. Instead of going through the problems with Jesus as my guide, I thought that I could handle them on my own if only God would heal my entire body instantly. I didn't want to depend on Him completely as He wanted me to.

In my spirit, I heard the Father whisper, "Look only to Me. I am always with you."

His voice ushered me across another bridge toward maturity. It was a difficult bridge, one that wobbled and threatened to toss me downward onto rocks of despair and resignation. But He was with me, and He would continue to be with me. As I crossed the bridge, I learned that God answers some prayers immediately, but sometimes He calls on us to wait them out, to trust for the answer, to cling faithfully. *God,* I prayed, *give me strength to wait this one out with You.*

I looked over at Dad with renewed faith. "Okay, Dad. It's another commercial. Let's go again."

During the next few months as winter thawed into spring, I was more content. I had accepted the fact that for a little longer God was asking me to walk out my healing. Nonetheless, I knew I could never be satisfied with my healing uncompleted. I would not release my grip on the promise that God would finish the work He had started. But for the moment, I was caught up in the spring rush of school activities, concentrating on making the best grades I could. For the time being, I shelved the question of my healing.

But I pulled the healing question from the shelf as the senior prom and graduation approached. My heart ached when I thought about the prom. I was like any other teenage girl. I wanted to go to the prom. I wanted to date. Spending every Friday and Saturday at home or at a ball game with my family was a constant reminder of my difference. The only guys I was ever around, besides those at school, were my brothers and the fellows in the youth group, who considered me their pal, their "neat friend." No matter how I would flirt and tease them with "Hey, good-looking!" I don't think the thought ever registered that I might be date material. No, I was a "sister in the Lord."

Desiree saw my sad eyes whenever someone mentioned the prom. My silence told her how I felt.

"Jama, why don't *you* ask someone to go with you? Lots of girls ask guys, especially if the guy goes to another school or has gone to college."

We were eating lunch. I bounced my spoon against the still Jell-O.

"I don't know, Desiree."

"You can ask a friend, maybe someone from the youth group. We could double. Come on, it'd be fun."

"But Desiree, I wouldn't be able to dance."

"So what? Half the people there last year didn't dance. They have tables set up, and you can sit and talk and hear the band. They have drinks and food. You don't have to dance. But, I bet you could slow dance." She winked.

I laughed, "I'd probably step on his feet though."

"Well, think about it. You can't miss your senior prom."

"But who would want to go with *me?*"

"Now, knock it off. Nothing's wrong with you. You're lots of fun, and more guys should know that."

Suddenly, she had that look on her face that always accompanied dangerous thoughts in her head. "Hey, why don't you ask Rick? He's a good friend, and we'd all have a fantastic time!"

Rick was a year older and in my brother Steve's class. During my junior year, I had seen a lot of him since he had started coming to the youth group. We also had the same study hall, and he and Steve were both on the wrestling team. I thought Rick was gorgeous with his dark hair and muscular build. He was a special friend, always treating me like a lady.

"Hmmm, maybe I *could* ask him. He's not dating anyone now, nobody that I know of anyway."

"You can call his mom and get his number at college," Desiree encouraged. Her eyes were like little lights.

"Okay, okay. I guess it couldn't hurt. We would have a good time, wouldn't we?" Her eyes ignited mine, and I could hardly wait for school's dismissal bell so I could go home and call Rick.

But Rick couldn't go. He said that he was really disappointed. I understood. He had other plans that he couldn't cancel. It wasn't that he didn't want to go with me, he had said. However, it was still a rejection. A sigh of resignation went straight through me. I would have given up and not tried to ask anyone else if Desiree had not persisted.

"Okay, okay," I told her.

And so I decided to call Al, who was in college in Illinois. Although we had gone to different high schools, we had remained friends. I hadn't seen him much since he'd been away at school, and he was surprised to hear from me. I was even more surprised when he said yes! I had to ask him to repeat his answer to make sure I had heard him correctly. He said yes both times!

I smiled continuously for the next two weeks. I was actually going to the prom. Mom teased me about being so cooperative and agreeable. She made me a beautiful, soft yellow dress with white eyelet sleeves. Al and I would meet Desiree and her date, Dave, at a friend's house for dinner before the prom, and another friend had invited us to watch old movies afterward on a screen her dad had set up on their lawn. Then we would all go someplace for breakfast. I didn't have to be home until six—six in the morning!

Not being able to dance didn't make any difference; I knew we would have a great time, just as Desiree had said.

But we didn't have a great time, because we didn't go. The morning of the prom, I woke up sicker than I had been in years. I thought for certain that I would be well enough to go. Mom and Dad prayed for me, I took a bath, washed my hair, and even got dressed. But I had a fever and was so weak that smiling was a great effort. After Al had given me my corsage, and I had given him his boutonniere, Dad took pictures of us. Then I had to go to bed. I was so sick that I couldn't think about being disappointed. But as I fell asleep I told myself, *At least you were going, at least you were going.*

Al spent the evening, dressed in suit and boutonniere, watching television with my family. I slept, too tired to be unhappy.

I didn't question why I had gotten sick at such an inopportune time. I would have liked to have gone to the prom, but just knowing that I *could* have gone, that I had plans to go, lessened the disappointment.

Up until then, graduation had been far away, neatly tucked in a corner called the future. After the prom, however, it sprang up, surprising me, scaring me, like the jack-in-the-box toy used to when I was a child. Now graduation was only three weeks away, and one after the other, the May days flew by. Again I pleaded with God to fulfill His complete healing in me. I wanted to walk across that auditorium stage to receive my diploma without a crutch. I rationalized and presented my case logically before God: *Wouldn't it be a marvelous testimony for You, Lord, if I walked up the stairs and across the stage and accepted my diploma totally healed? Wouldn't the people know that it was Your power that did the healing since they know how severely I was injured?* But my motive wasn't to glorify God. I was driven by the desire to be another normal student and not so different. I was bargaining. I was putting my own will above His will, and I knew it.

Mom had an open house for friends and relatives on the Sunday evening before graduation on Tuesday evening. I had to respond with the same, "I don't know," to everyone's questions about my future. I had been accepted at Ball State, but wasn't sure what

major to declare. I had numbed my mind to the reality of graduation and going to Ball State—until May 28, 1974.

Sitting on the stage with the class officers and those who were
giving speeches, I saw the reality in the rows and rows of blue-
gowned seniors. I couldn't see my family in the mass of friends and
relatives. After three students had given speeches, the principal
came to the podium to begin the roll call. "Please hold your
applause until the end of the ceremony so that it will move more
quickly," he said. As the alphabetical roll call continued, I saw
Desiree walk across and receive her diploma. She was a *J,* and I
was a *K!* The hollowness in the pit of my stomach moved through
my body, until I felt like a shell sitting in the chair. My hands were
limp in my lap.

"Jama Kehoe," I heard from the podium. The auditorium was
silent. Two friends sitting in the row with me, Don, the class
president, and Terry, a top student, came over and, placing their
hands on my elbows, helped me to my feet. I walked slowly across
the stage, looking neither to the right, nor to the left. The only
sounds I heard were my new shoes against the wood floor. The
distance seemed longer than it had in practice, and the quiet
stretched time out of proportion. Reaching the podium, I shook
the principal's hand.

"Congratulations, Jama," he said. His grin was wide.

"Congratulations," the superintendent of schools repeated.

"Thank you," I looked away from their eyes: I felt the heat of
hundreds of eyes on me, and I wanted to get back to my seat. I
handed Terry my diploma and slipped my arm through his bent
elbow again, as the three of us walked past the table of diplomas
to circle around back to my chair. The silence was shattered, like
fragile crystal, by the explosive clapping of many hands. I was
nearly immobilized by surprise. People all over the auditorium
rose to their feet.

"What *are* they doing?" I muttered to Don and Terry. "They're
not supposed to do that."

"You deserve it," Terry said.

I couldn't look at the audience. If I let my concentration shift from my walking to the reality of the ceremony, I knew I would cry.

Terry and Don helped me to my seat, and I watched the rest of the seniors parade past to receive diplomas. The roll call ended.

"Will the senior class of 1974 please rise."

I retrieved the crutch from under the row of chairs, put my diploma and program on the chair beside me, and quickly worked to get leverage so I could stand with my classmates for the changing of the tassels. I stood and adjusted my robe.

"You are now graduates of Northside High School," I heard. Throughout the auditorium was a rustling as tassels were moved from left to right, then shouting, then clapping. I sighed, and weakly smiled. High school was over, and I was scared because I didn't know in what direction my life would be going.

12

Pumping and Steering

"Get it yourself, Jama." Doug's words weren't mean, but they surprised me. I hadn't asked him to get me anything extraordinary, just a glass of pop. I was hot and thirsty from lying in the June sun.

One small laugh escaped, maybe he was kidding. "Well, Doug, gosh . . ." I stuttered. He would usually get me anything I wanted.

"I know. I know." He pulled the bread from the bread drawer. "I could get it for you. But you can get it yourself. Besides, I'm in a hurry; I've got to make a sandwich and get back to work."

"Okay, never mind. I guess I'm not that thirsty." But I was. He ignored my silent pouting as I sat at the table and watched him eat. He didn't get me the glass of pop. I had thought he might after he finished making his sandwich.

"See you later." He plopped his painting hat on his head and dashed out the screen door. My "bye" was barely audible.

"It was only a glass of Coke," I muttered. "No one else is home, and it would have been so much *easier* if he would have gotten the drink for me."

I sat there, getting thirstier. I knew Doug was right. I got up, found a bottle of pop in the refrigerator and began the struggle.

For fifteen minutes I battled with bottle opener and bottle. The right combination of pressure and leverage seemed impossible to coordinate. My frustration level was rising. I was ready to burst into tears, but a vent of determination released some of the pressure.

I'm not going to let this dumb bottle get the best of me, I vowed.

My anger must have injected strength into my hands because I heard a pop and the top flipped onto the counter. It was one of the best tasting drinks I had ever had. Standing at the counter, I gulped down half of it; then with my crutch in one hand and the glass in the other, I walked to the table and sat down. I sat and thought about my attitude.

I shouldn't have treated Doug the way I did when he denied me the drink. He hadn't said it to be heartless. He just didn't think that I had to be waited on all the time. He was more right than he probably knew. Someone had to say it sooner or later. I should realize that the no from Doug and the no's from the rest of the family were said out of love, a love that wanted to see me progress.

A few days before graduation, I had made the decision to go to Ball State, and Dad wanted me to live on campus. If I was going to do that, then I would have to learn to do more for myself than I was doing. Everyone else could do what I tried to do in one-tenth the time, but getting indignant about their no's was childish. In saying no, they were saying yes. Yes to my progress. Yes to my maturity.

I wanted to say yes to being more independent, but I didn't know if I was ready to say yes to living on campus. Long after my drink of pop was gone, I sat at the table, thinking about high school, about college, and about my future. Dad came in, startling me back to the present.

"Here, I picked this up for you." He tossed a book on the table. The red symbol for handicapped was on the front; under the symbol it said, Ball State University.

"What's this for?"

"I didn't know this, but Ball State is one of the best schools in the state in providing facilities for handicapped students. I thought you might want to look this book over. It tells all about the facilities in the dorms."

The dorms. "Oh, Dad. I don't know about living in a dorm."

"I know. We've talked about it already. But I think it would be good for you. You'd make so many friends and feel more a part of college. Now, I'm not trying to get rid of you, you know." He sat down at the table and squeezed my leg at the knee in a ticklish spot. He had done that to me since I was a little kid; he knew it would make me laugh.

"Cut it out, Dad." I pushed his hand away. I didn't want to

laugh. This decision was too serious. "I know it would probably be good for me, and I'd love it if I never had to get out and go to classes. But how am I supposed to get around once I'm there? You know how long it takes me to get anywhere. I couldn't even make it around Northside on time. I was always tardy to my classes." I couldn't keep the whine out of my voice.

"Well, I've been doing a lot of thinking about that. Remember that three-wheeled bicycle Grandma had when we were down in Florida over Christmas? I was thinking about the possibility of you riding one. I think you could do it. You ride the stationary bike here at home."

I remembered that bicycle. It looked like a tractor.

Dad continued while I remained silent. "If you rode the bike around campus, then living in a dorm would put you a lot closer to your classes." I saw fatherly love in his eyes. "I called a couple of places about the bikes, and I thought we might go out to one of them tomorrow to try one out. What do you think?"

"I guess we could try it out. It *would* be good exercise, wouldn't it?"

Dad grinned, reached over and massaged my shoulder as I kept telling myself to think positive. "Now that's the way to talk! It sure would be!" Without my saying a word, Dad knew I was saying yes to living in a dorm on campus. He didn't push me, but his gentle nudgings were firm. It was time for me to move out of the nest. He pulled a housing contract out of his shirt pocket, and together we filled it out.

Three days later, a blue, three-wheeled bicycle was delivered to our house. As I looked at the huge thing sitting in our driveway, it definitely reminded me of a tractor. When I had gone to the bicycle shop to try riding it, it was very awkward. But I knew if I practiced all summer, I would have better control by the opening of school in September.

To mount the bike, I had to grip the hand brake with my right hand, put my left hand on the handlebar, and then scoot my body up on the seat. I always had to mount from the same side, because my right leg was stronger than my left and it was easier to lift it over the bar and chain guard. And my shoes had to have heels to keep my feet from sliding off the pedals when I rode. I had to leave the crutch at home while I rode, until Dad got the idea to screw a metal broom holder on the bar under the seat. The crutch then snapped into it, parallel to the road.

I rode every day. At first with Mom and Dad, going only a few blocks; then alone, sometimes for as long as two hours. My stamina, endurance, and speed increased. I had to stop less and less to readjust my feet on the pedals. As I pedaled along backcountry roads behind our house, I prayed that the Lord would keep building up my muscles. More and more I enjoyed riding the bike, even if it did look comical. The bike was so heavy that I couldn't speed on level roads; but going down hills, I loved hearing the whiz of air past my ears, feeling the warm wind on my face and through my hair.

One morning, Mom asked if I'd ride with her to the campus. She wanted to time how fast I could get from my dorm, across campus, to the other buildings. I agreed. I hadn't ridden that way very often because I had to cross four lanes of traffic. Mom was easy to ride with because she liked to go slowly, and that was the only speed my bike had: slow. We talked and rode; I loved being with Mom. I still avoided thinking about how much I depended on her and how I would manage in the dorm.

The dorm I was going to live in, Botsford Hall, was the farthest away from the main campus, but it was the honor dorm and I wanted to live there. Mom timed me with her watch. In ten minutes I pedaled up to the English building. Since I had decided to major in English, I would be spending many class hours in that building. A big hill curved up and around to the front entrance.

"Think you can make it up that?" she nodded.

"There's only one way to find out. Come on."

I began pumping. And I pumped, and I pumped. I had to apply the brakes halfway up to stop and catch my breath.

"You okay?" asked Mom as she pumped beside me. I didn't have enough extra breath to speak. I nodded.

Pump, puff, pump, puff. Finally reaching the top, I felt like "the little engine that could." We rested. I wanted to lie down and go to sleep.

"Whew! Praise the Lord!" gasped Mom. "You're stronger than I thought. I could barely make that one."

Still winded, I just nodded again. We were quiet for a while, feeling the morning sun burn toward noon.

"You ready to head home before it gets much hotter?" Mom finally asked.

"Yes, we better go now. My energy is melting."

We circled the English building, rode across the street, and went up the bicycle ramps, toward home. We talked more: about missing Steve while he spent the summer as a counselor at a golf camp, about the craft projects I had been working on to sell at the end of the summer for money to buy school clothes.

Then, with the mention of school, Mom asked, "Don't you think it would be a good idea for Dad to get you one of those orange flags to put on the back of your bike? I saw a young boy on a three-wheeler the other day and he had one It would be a good idea since you'll be in more traffic, don't you think?" She was really serious. We turned into the driveway, and I started laughing.

"Mom, honestly, don't you think I'm conspicuous enough? I mean, look at the size of this thing." I was laughing so hard that I could barely pedal the few feet up to the front of the house. Mom started to chuckle, too.

"Come to think of it, I guess they would see the bike before they would see the flag."

"It would have to be a pretty good-sized flag, that's for sure."

"Okay, okay, so forget the flag idea." We were still chuckling when we walked into the house.

As much as I enjoyed riding with others, riding alone was my one escape, the only time I had control of where I wanted to go. Since I couldn't get in the car and just drive, I got on my bike and just rode. I needed time alone; I needed time to think.

Saying yes to college life in the dorm was a big mental and emotional step. There were still so many things I couldn't do that members of my family did for me: When I lost my balance and fell, I couldn't get up without help. When I came to curbs or steps without railings, I needed a balancing hand. My arms and hands weren't strong enough to carry anything heavy. I couldn't get out of the bathtub by myself. I knew where I had been, and I rejoiced in where God had brought me, but I wondered if it was too early to be stepping out from my protective fortress of family security.

Riding alone day after day, I began accepting that I had committed myself to the dormitory housing contract. Just as Doug had told me at the beginning of the summer to get the pop myself, I knew I had to think of substitute ways in which I could do the things others had always done for me. I developed a whole new attitude: I had to be less selfish, less demanding on my family.

I was torn between wanting them to help me because it was easier and wanting to be independent because I wasn't a child anymore. I could wash my hair in the sink. I had never tried to stand in the tub for a shower, but if the dorm had stalls, maybe I could stand and shower then. I would just have to be observant and park the bike close to the building, over the curbs. It was the same with the steps, I would have to notice which steps had railings and which didn't. And if I picked up my feet when I was walking, and concentrated and prayed, my stumbles would be less.

On every bike ride, during every quiet time, and before falling asleep every night, I thought about what might or might not happen. When the little computer of my mind wore down and couldn't analyze hypothetical situations anymore, I knew I had to surrender myself once again into the hands of God. I had exhausted myself by thinking *I* would be able to work out whatever I came against.

I probed my heart. Where did I get my strength? From the Lord who made heaven and earth. Where was my faith? In the Lord who made impossibilities possible. The promise I had lost sight of came into view again: He would never leave me. The live power of that promise sent a new surge of hope. I would not be alone in the dorm, in my classes, in the cafeteria, anywhere. *He promised.*

The bicycle gave me a new freedom. I was more mobile than I had been since the accident. I hadn't thought I would be able to ride a bicycle until I was completely healed. Finding out I could was a nice surprise even though the bike wasn't a ten-speed. And then, one morning in mid-June, I discovered another nice surprise that I thought wouldn't be possible until I had full muscle control.

I was sitting at the kitchen table reading the morning paper, procrastinating about my work on the craft projects I had to finish. Mom was cleaning the kitchen. The telephone rang and Mom answered it.

"Just a minute." She held her hand over the receiver. "It's for you. A man."

She stood beside me after I took the phone. She was as curious as I was. Men just didn't call me.

"Hello. This is Jama." I listened as he talked. As my eyes grew bigger and bigger and I gasped, Mom kept whispering, "What? What?"

"Yes!" I shouted before realizing that I had. "Of course I'm interested! When?" My enthusiasm rippled across the wires. I continued to listen to him explain, ignoring Mom, blocking out everything but his words.

"Thank you," I said when he finished. "Thank you very much. You'll call when you're ready? Okay? Bye. And thanks."

"Will you please tell me what's going on? Who was that? What did he want? What are you interested in?"

"Well you little eavesdropper!" I teased her.

"Oh Jama, tell me. Come on. I'm your mother." Her pleadings were irresistible. I couldn't keep the smile from my face.

"Get ready, Mom, you'll never believe this. I didn't, but that was Mr. Mihal, and I'm going to learn to drive a *car!*"

"A car?" She sat down. "You're kidding? Tell me what he said."

I was glad to tell her. I wanted to tell the world! I had always been a little envious when all my friends had received their drivers' licenses. Any time I wanted to go anywhere, I had to rely on someone to take me. It would be great to say to Desiree, *"I'll* pick *you* up."

"The car works with hand controls, Mom. Some man who is handicapped donated it to Ball State's Driver's Education Department. I think I'll have to see it to completely understand how it works, but he said that a metal plate is placed over the gas pedal, and something's done to the brake. And then all that is connected to a hand-operated lever that goes underneath the steering wheel and sticks out beside the turn signal. He said that by pulling down on the lever, I stop the car, and by pushing it forward, I accelerate it. Everything's done with the hands. Sounds pretty neat, doesn't it? Oh, and there's a knob on the steering wheel, so I can turn the car easier."

"I didn't even know such equipment was available. Just think, Jama behind the wheel! When do you start your lessons?" She was shaking her head in disbelief.

"Something has to be fixed in the car, so he said it may be a few days. But he wanted to make sure that I was interested. Gee, who's he kidding? Who wouldn't want to drive?"

I didn't want to leave the house in case Mr. Mihal called. Day after day as I waited for the phone to ring, my eagerness came through my fingers, and I got more accomplished than ever. I produced miniature oil paintings, three-dimensional plaques, small crewelwork canvases.

Ten days later the call finally came. Mom dropped me off at the Driver's Education building on campus, right across from Botsford Hall. It was a building I had never noticed before, even though Mom and I had ridden past it often on our bikes. Nervousness inched its way over my body. I had waited anxiously for this, but confidence was oozing away rapidly. I had conquered my ponderous three-wheel bike, but would I be able to control something as big as a car?

"Here's the car," Mr. Mihal said. He had been waiting in the parking lot. Mom honked as she pulled into the street. I waved. She was probably praying as hard as I was.

"I'll drive over to the stadium parking lot and then give you the wheel." He winked. He was a family friend, and I was glad that someone who knew me would be teaching me.

I drove in small circles around the parking lot to get the feel of the controls. He said that becoming adjusted to them would be easier for me than for those who had learned how to drive with their feet and then had to switch to hand controls. The controls were sensitive, especially the brake. The car leaped like a big frog until I practiced pulling and pushing the lever with the right amount of pressure. The nervousness I had about controlling a car evaporated; I knew I was going to be a good driver.

Mr. Mihal took me out in the car twice a week. As soon as I received my learner's permit, I graduated from the parking lot to country roads, to residential areas, to main streets, to downtown, to highway. Each time I drove, my confidence solidified. I enjoyed driving. With both hands occupied, I had to learn different ways to turn on the windshield wipers and the radio. One approach was to wait until I came to a red light or stop sign, when my right hand could be free from the steering wheel. The other method was a bit more daring: With the car moving, I could move my left hand from the control lever to the steering wheel, then turn the necessary knobs with my right hand. With the second method, the car would gradually slow, because I wasn't pulling on the accelerator, but I learned to change quickly so I didn't slow down much.

Learning to drive was exciting. However, I knew that I wouldn't be able to take my driver's examination until our family had hand controls installed in our car. And because any car that I drove had to have power steering and power brakes, Dad would have to trade in our second car which had neither. Although I dreamed of having a car on campus instead of my three-wheeler bike, I was being unrealistic, because I knew that our family couldn't afford to buy me my own car. But just the thought that I would have access to a car if I needed it, that *I* could drive it, was elating.

Until we could get a car equipped with the controls so I could be tested for my operator's license, I never missed a lesson with Mr. Mihal. I would ride the bike over to the lot where *my* car was parked, enjoy an hour and a half of new independence, and then be patient.

"You're not nervous about me driving on the road, are you, Dad?" I asked him one day after I had returned from driving.

"Well, I'd rather have you *on* the road than driving *off* the road!"

"Oh, Dad," I giggled. "But really, you'll have to come with me sometime to see how I handle the hand controls."

"Me? In the same car with you? With you *driving?*" His teasing eyes lit up with love.

"You just wait. I may be driving in the Indy "500" one of these days. That is, if I can find one of those race cars with hand controls on it!" He laughed and hugged me.

13
The Date

I wonder what my roommate will be like? I wonder if she'll like me? I wonder if she'll be wild or if she'll be a Christian? Will it matter to her that I walk with a crutch?

I had surrendered, or tried to surrender, all the anxiety I had about living in a college dorm. As for the worry about mobility around campus and a definite area of study, the Lord had crumbled it with His mighty hand: I was riding the bike, and I was majoring in English. But I couldn't totally surrender my worry about a roommate. I knew God wanted to crumble that problem, too, but He had to wait for me.

I wanted to be confident. I wanted to be secure. I wanted to know that this step was the will of God. My mind knew the Scripture "Do not worry or be anxious about tomorrow" (*see* Matthew 6:37). But, I couldn't relinquish my own will into His control. My heart was feeble, and I couldn't have victory or comfort about my roommate until I gave up the fight, released my grasp on worry, and gave Him control.

I moved into Botsford Hall on a Sunday morning. As Mom and I walked up to the front desk to ask about my room assignment, I realized that we hadn't thought about coming over to the hall to check out the living situation. We knew that the dorm was open during the summer for summer school, but for some reason, the idea of coming into the hall to see the different floors and the layout of the building didn't enter our minds.

But I didn't let that bother me. God was in control and He would take care of it. I had to remember that He knew what was best for me, that He knew what I had need of before I asked Him.

And take care of me He did. He was guiding my steps and leading me. When He led me into Botsford Hall, He led me to the first floor, to a room right across from the restrooms which had a shower equipped with a seat. He led me to a Christian roommate and to special neighbors. He led me to the artesian well of answers, answers to the prayers that I had asked in faith, believing.

My roommate was Denise. She was petite and all smiles and blue eyes. During those first few months, our friendship was a tender, fragile yearling. Throughout the year, it often stumbled or fell and was hurt; but then, it would rise again to romp and frolic and be happy. The falls we had only hurt because we really cared; the fun we had was magnified by teasing and laughter.

Other bonds of friendship were also created. Donna, who lived next door, stole a part of my heart. She was one of those rare persons who could make one feel very positive. She saw beyond the crutch, beyond the physical differences, and established her friendship with my heart. Ours was not a surface friendship that would dissolve with time or distance, it was a forever one.

The school year always seems so contradictory: Time seems to move slowly and yet so fast. I became adjusted to school, to living without my family, although we still saw and talked to each other often. Every Sunday, they would come to the dorm to pick me up for church, and I would go home with them afterward for our traditional Sunday dinner.

Steve was a sophomore at BSU and on the volleyball team. Frequently, he would stop by the dorm on his way home from practice just to see how I was doing. The other girls on the floor always peeked in the door when he was there. They constantly talked about how cute he was and pestered me to get him to ask them out.

Julee also loved to ride her bike over to be in the "college atmosphere." At thirteen she looked very mature, and I saw many of the guys give her a double take, which thrilled her. Dad loved it when I invited him to the dining service for lunches, and I often called him when I had a problem, like my tires going flat or the chain falling off the bike. He helped me when he knew I couldn't handle the situation alone. But when I asked him to help me buy the many books for my English classes, he said I could go to the bookstore and get them myself. I pouted a little, knowing how heavy the books were, but I did get them myself. And afterward, I felt proud that I had done it.

Of course, Mom seemed to be the one to visit the dorm more than anyone in the family. She would make my favorite chocolate chip cookies and bring them to me and Denise. Almost every girl on the first floor knew my whole family. They joked that I was lucky to have them so close. Mom also helped me with the laundry, since I wasn't strong enough yet to carry the laundry basket even the short distance across the hall to the washing machine. But that help only lasted for my freshman year. My independence increased, and so did my appreciation of my family.

Yet, even with my adjustment to college, I was not a natural cog to fit into the secular machine. My naiveté jutted obstrusively from my sheltered adolescence. As a Christian cog, I was tested and hammered at unconsciously to adapt to the standards of the worldly machine, to believe what it believed. I couldn't rely on my family to be the buffer against the hammer. I had to put up my own shield. I knew what was right and wrong, and I had to make my own choice about the kind of cog I wanted to be.

The pressure concerning smoking, drinking, and sexual relationships challenged my naive ideals as they never had been challenged in high school. I had not been blind to everything that went on at Northside, but the friends with whom I spent the most time all believed in the standards and principles of the Bible as their guide for moral behavior. Now, I had a variety of friends who had a variety of beliefs. I made the decision to be the Christian cog I had been brought up to be. I wanted to fit into God's machine, into the Body of Christ. I prayed that I wouldn't hide my light under any bushels. I wanted my new friends in the dorm and in my classes to see Christ in me, to know I moved in His love, by His power.

But this decision was not always evident. Frustrations, fears, and confusion about classes, grades, dating, and being accepted crept in and threw a bushel over my light. I didn't know if the love of Christ that had been shed in my heart was penetrating. People were curious about me, wanting to know what had happened, and I shared what the power of prayer and the power of God would do in a life when medical science didn't offer much hope. As I did so, I rejoiced afresh in the victories He had given; nonetheless, I had an unspoken disappointment that they could not see a total healing in me. I didn't know if this disappointment could be heard in my voice.

I had an inner joy, the joy of salvation, the joy of God's love, which no one could take from me. However, this joy did not always surface. I had the joy that is based in God's steadfastness. But happiness is based on human emotions and circumstances, and I could not always be happy with my circumstances. I could not be happy when my friends did things I wanted to do, but wasn't able. I put on the happy mask, but I was not completely happy. The pouting, self-centered child stomped in. I wanted to enjoy college life as a total, normal person. I wanted to be free from the burden of working around my limitations as I performed the simplest everyday activities.

I wanted to just go, without wondering, *Can I walk there? Will my bike go there? How much extra time do I have to allow?* I felt cheated because I couldn't run across the Ball State campus to the tennis courts or the dances with my friends. I became locked again in the sad cage of thinking I was an embarrassment because I had to ride that bike and because I walked so slowly.

So, whenever I wanted to do something on campus, like see a movie, or a play, or go to a show at the auditorium, I suppressed the idea of asking and waited to be asked. I didn't want anyone to feel obligated to go anywhere with me. I was different and that terrible difference reerected the wall of inferiority I thought I had broken down during high school.

Denise saw the hurt the wall produced. Late one night, after we had turned out the light to go to bed, it seemed as though she could hear me lying there, thinking and hurting.

"Jama, what's the matter?" she asked gently. "I'll listen if you want to talk."

I wasn't used to opening my heart to expose my fears and struggles. My feelings were too frail. Brick upon brick I had

mortared a wall around the fragile, timid child inside me. Before
I answered, I asked myself, *How would exposing my hurts reflect
upon my Christian witness?* Wasn't I supposed to lean on Jesus as
my strength? Wasn't Jesus supposed to carry my loads? How
could I burden someone else with my load? Would she think I was
a weak Christian when I told her that I, too, hurt and struggled?

I was confident and secure in the love of my family; no walls
were built between us. But I was entering into new relationships,
and I yearned to be understood and accepted. I was afraid of being
unloved and rejected because of my weaknesses.

Cloaked in the darkness, my face and my pain were hidden from
scrutiny. "Well," I paused.

"If you don't want to tell me, that's okay. But, let me tell you,
friends are for listening."

"I'm just so tired of studying and studying and not making the
grades I want. And I'm doing worse in English than I've ever done
before; I've always gotten A's and now I'm not. I'm tired of riding
that bike around. It looks like a tractor, and I'm embarrassed.
And I want to date so badly. But who's going to ask out a girl who
rides a tricycle? I thought the guys in college would be more
mature and accepting than those in high school, but they're not.
I'd really like to quit, I'm so frustrated."

My sentences were strung together in a chain of disappointment. The words were as negative and as dark as the night into
which they were spoken. I had held inside the disappointment
about not being completely healed. I didn't want sympathy. I
didn't want lectures about immaturity and impatience. I wanted
to be heard, to be cared about. I wanted to be assured that whether
I failed or succeeded, whether I was attractive or repulsive, I was
still loved.

After I spoke and after the silence, I thought, *Now what is poor
Denise supposed to say in answer to a speech like that?* But her
words spoke peace, comfort, encouragement.

"Jama, I'm not sure what to say, or what you want me to say,
so I'll just say what's on my mind. This is our freshman year.
Everybody says that it's always the hardest. But you're smart, and
so what if you don't make straight A's? You're just getting used

to how to study. It's hard for me, too, but we'll make it. You've got your family to support you, and you've got me here, and Donna next door, and your other friends.

"And don't worry about the bike," she continued. "People admire you more than you know, and they don't think you're funny looking. As for guys, they're a big hassle! If I were you, I'd just wait until some guy rides up on a white horse to sweep you away!"

I laughed. "Yes, I wish he'd come soon. Before final examinations would be a pretty good time, wouldn't it?"

She laughed, too, and the fact that she cared enough to ask and to listen sent a message of love straight through my wall. The crack wasn't wide, but it was there. For now, that was enough. Her message brought fresh strength and courage.

I began studying even harder to prove to myself that I had the intelligence to succeed in college. But just as I decided to think less about dating, a guy in my geography class asked me out! I thought he was talking to the girl next to me. He had to ask me twice. I said yes before thinking logically about it, I was so taken by surprise. I didn't even ask myself, *Is he a Christian?*

I had asked God for dates with Christian guys since I was a sophomore in high school. I had been telling God that I didn't have to be asked out every weekend, or even date steadily, that I would be happy to go out with guys just as friends. Then, when I wasn't asked out by Christians, I told God that I would settle for non-Christians.

"Send me pagans, I'll witness to them and convert them," I bargained.

I didn't really want to date non-Christians, but I was feeling desperate. I feared I would never date and be an old maid. I wanted to feel desirable, to know that I was liked by the opposite sex.

Denise and Donna wanted to meet him when he came to pick me up, but they were both going home for the weekend, and their rides left before he arrived. I had instructions to give them detailed reports when they returned Sunday evening. Late Friday afternoon, he came to Botsford to pick me up. We talked for a while and then walked through the lounge, out the double doors, and into the warmth of the late autumn afternoon. Then I saw the motorcycle parked on the sidewalk, an enormous thing. It was his!

"Think you can mount this baby?" he asked.

I looked at him and then back at the bike. It looked bigger the second time. I laughed a shallow, insecure laugh. I didn't want to look scared. *Oh, dear God,* I prayed, *what have I gotten myself into?*

I tried another laugh, an "Oh-I-do-this-all-the-time" laugh. I hoped it was believable. "I may need a boost. That's some bike." His eyes showed pride of ownership.

"Sure is!" he agreed. "Let me put the helmet on you." He placed it on my head, and I thought my legs would buckle under me it was so heavy. And so large. I wondered who's head it was supposed to fit.

"Hey, who turned out the lights!" I thought I heard my voice echo in the cavern of helmet.

He laughed. "Here, let me adjust that." When he lifted the helmet up, and I could see again, I couldn't believe it. Walking up the sidewalk toward us was my father! I had told my parents that I was going out—I wanted to tell everybody I knew—but I didn't think anyone would "drop by" to see the guy. Dad looked as if he couldn't believe what he saw: his little girl, all helmet, standing beside a guy over six feet tall, and a motorcycle.

As I made the proper introductions, Dad kept staring. He stared at what he could see of me, at the guy, at the bike. He handed me a check that had come in the mail.

"Thought you might need this." His voice sounded so unnatural that I thought he was in shock. His eyes constantly shifted.

"Thanks, Dad." I put the check in my jeans pocket. We all stood there, in silence.

"Well, I guess I'd better be going. Your mother is in the car. Nice meeting you." He nodded; they both shook hands. *Please Dad, don't say, "Take care of my little girl,"* I thought.

"Nice to meet you, too, sir." And then *he* said it! "I'll take care of your daughter."

I thought I heard a small laugh from Dad, but I wasn't certain. And then, peering from beneath the helmet, I watched him walk back to the car.

One boost and I was up on the bike. But what to do with the crutch? I held it across my lap with one hand, wrapped my other arm tightly across his body and prayed, *God, help me to hold on. Be with me, O God, O Jesus,* I pleaded. My legs pressed in toward the seat; my one arm clung to him. *Oh courage, where are you?* I asked.

The faster the bike went, the faster my heart beat. But the roar of the engine deafened the thumping of the heart. As he turned onto River Road, I looked down, down to the river, almost a straight drop from the road. My heart dropped down, down into the pit of my stomach. *Surely he doesn't want to go down there,* I hoped. Oh yes, he did.

On the way from road to riverside, I concentrated all my strength on clinging. We bounced and bumped all the way. My mind was saying, *Jesus, Jesus,* but my teeth were so clenched I could speak no words. We made level ground. I wanted to sing, to kiss the dirt, but instead every part of me sighed in relief. I looked back up the hill we had come down. It wasn't a hill. It was a mountain!

He helped me off the bike, and we walked to the bank of the river.

"Wasn't that fun?" he smiled as he helped me sit down.

My nod and yes were feeble attempts at affirmation.

The sun started to drop behind the forest of black, pencil-thin trees, and its orange hues made the black blacker. I felt uncomfortable. He had his arms around me as we talked. Outwardly, the hug felt nice; he was gentle and natural. Inwardly, I felt something was wrong, awkward. We really didn't know each other.

As the sun went down, the air chilled. I was feeling more and more uncomfortable and wanted to leave. I was not only getting cold, I was getting hungry. I finally convinced him that it was time to get something to eat. But then I remembered that we had to go up the mountain we had come down. He helped me onto the bike again; then he got on. From the bottom, the hill looked even steeper.

"Hang on," he said.

Is he crazy? I thought. *Of course I'm going to hang on.* "You bet," I agreed.

"This is awfully steep. I hope we can get up it. I usually make it when I'm by myself. I hope the extra weight doesn't pull us down."

Gee, thanks, I thought. I couldn't tell if he was teasing or not. I softly chuckled, hoping that he was. "Yes, I hope it doesn't either."

He revved up the motor. I clung tightly, leaning forward, thinking that my weight might help the motorcycle go upward better. The bike lurched. I kept my eyes looking ahead at the incline. Halfway up the engine died.

I didn't have time to scream. The helmet came down over my eyes, and I felt my body hit the ground. The bike was on top of me. I knew it weighed two tons.

"My bike!" I heard him scream, pulling on the handlebars to lift it.

"Your bike! What about me?" I was smashed between the hard ground and the heavy bike.

"Oh. Are you okay?" He was adjusting the rearview mirror. I was wiped out, and he was checking to see if his bike was hurt! I couldn't believe what I was seeing. Physically, I wasn't hurt, but I thought, *Of all the nerve!*

"Yes, I'm okay. But you'll have to help me up, please." He lifted me to my feet and handed me the crutch. It was smashed together so my arm wouldn't fit through the metal cylinder. The screws were still tight, so I pulled the cylinder apart.

"I think maybe we'll have to go down the road a bit where the hill isn't so steep. You're all right, aren't you? I tried to catch the bike before it fell."

"I know. Yes, I'm fine. I'm pretty tough." I laughed. It was a little funny when I thought about how it must have looked. We weren't hurt, and the bike only had a slightly bent mirror.

Up on the bike once more, we found a smoother place to ride

up. As we started up that time, I closed my eyes and prayed. When I opened them, the lurching movement had stopped; we were back on River Road! I wanted to sigh, but thought that if I did, I would let out all the strength I would need to hold on during the ride home. And I needed all the strength I could get, since he wanted to show me that he could get the bike to go from zero to eighty in fifteen seconds. We stopped at McDonald's and he asked me if I had any money. I handed him the few dollars I had stuffed in my pocket and then began to question how this date was going to end. When he came back from the counter with our hamburgers, he never said a word about the money, no mention of an IOU or anything. *This is not how I thought it was going to be,* I thought.

After we finished our hamburgers, he took me over to his dorm, the graduate students' dorm. Even after eating, my stomach felt empty. I was nervous. He wouldn't listen when I suggested going to my dorm. "It'll be quieter," he said.

Quieter for what? I wondered. I thought I knew what he had in mind and I wanted to go to Botsford where I felt safer, because I didn't have *that* in mind at all. We walked into the lounge on the third floor to watch television. It was empty. *Surely he won't try anything here, and at seven o'clock,* I told myself.

"Here, I'll put your crutch in the corner as soon as you sit down. You won't need it while we watch TV." I began wishing I had asked Desiree and Denise some more questions about how to act on a date. Maybe I wasn't ready to date after all. I sat down in a straight-backed chair; it looked the safest. That way he would have to sit in another chair. *No couch for this chicken,* I thought.

After we watched an hour or so of television, he said that he had something to show me. My eyes widened as he took off his shirt.

"Do you know much about kung fu?" he asked.

My hands were clammy. "No, not much. Only what I've seen on that television show."

"Allow me to demonstrate."

I relaxed a little as I watched him perform maneuvers he called *katas,* groaning and kicking and punching. I felt safe in the straight-backed chair. When he finished, I congratulated him on

his athletic ability and suggested that it was probably time to take
me back to the dorm. He was agreeable.

When we got to the dorm room, I wanted our good-bye to be
quick. He had told me during the evening that he was twenty-one
and had been in the Marines. I was inexperienced, and I wanted
to stay that way. But I made the mistake of allowing him into the
room. I sat down on the edge of my bed, while he told me a long
story about his life. The next thing I knew he was sitting beside
me. I felt utterly defenseless as he kissed me and pulled me back
on the bed. My power to resist couldn't begin to compete with his
kung fu-conditioned arms.

"No. No. Don't do that. I really think you should go."

"Don't you like this?"

"No. Please go." My no to everything was adamant.

"But I can lock the door."

"No."

"Let's make the evening good."

"It's been a good evening already. I had a nice time. But now
it's time for you to go. Please."

"Okay, okay."

I watched him as he closed the door. Then, alone, I collapsed
back on the bed totally exhausted; physically, from the bike ride,
and emotionally, from shouting no. If this was dating, then I guess
I could abstain a while longer. Lying on the bed, I stretched my
tense body.

There was a knock at the door. No, he wouldn't . . . "Who is
it?"

"It's Sue."

"Oh," I sighed. "Come on in."

"I heard the door shut and thought perhaps your date had left,
and I'm dying to know. How did it go?"

I took a deep breath and began recapping my first college date.
Laughter spilled from me and from Sue when I related my story
to her.

"Honest, that's the way it happened. And my dad coming and
McDonald's—sounds like it should be in a movie, doesn't it? The
moment that bike fell, I didn't think it was very funny, though.
But now . . ."

"Well, I told you I thought you were brave for accepting a date with a guy you didn't know very well, some guy you'd talked to only twice a week in geography class."

"Yes, I know. Well, so ends my first college date. I'm telling you, it may be the last if that's what they're all like. What an experience! I don't think I'm ready for all this!" The more I told her some of the things that happened, the more we laughed.

"I can't believe you went on a motorcycle!"

"I know. I bet my dad can't either. Think maybe I should trade in my bike for one?"

"Oh, I wish I could have seen you."

"It must have been a sight. Me on the back of a speeding motorcycle, holding a crutch that stuck out like a balancing pole on each side!"

Sue and I laughed and talked a while longer and then she left. When she had gone, I realized that God had really been looking out for me, but that I had to take some responsibility and maybe not be so quick to say yes when a guy asked me out. My over-friendly Marine had taught me that. *But you asked for it, Jama,* I thought. *You certainly did.*

14

The Ache of Anticipation

"It's for you, Jama," Denise said, her hand covering the receiver. "It's a *guy!*"

It had been six months since my friend with the motorcycle had asked me out, so I didn't think he would be calling after all this time. Denise giggled and handed me the phone. "It's not your brother," she sang.

I gave her a be-quiet look and said sweetly, "Hello."

"Hi! This is Mike."

My heart thumped and my mind envisioned strong, athletic Mike. During my senior year in high school, I had watched him play basketball against my high school's team in the big city rivalry. Although he hadn't come to our youth group, I knew that he was a Christian. We had met a couple of times and had mutual friends.

We talked on the phone for over an hour. It was good to hear that we had common opinions about sports, about our faith, about Christian fellowship. Mike's call caused my heart to applaud the spring. After the date with a non-Christian, I had wondered if all guys had a one-track mind when it came to girls? I had prayed, *Lord, why don't You bring a nice, Christian guy into my life? Let me see what it's like to go out with a guy who has the same standards that I have.*

I did go out with Mike. Our relationship was comfortable. We went to dinner, to Bible teachings. He called every few days and came to Botsford to visit me. Most of our conversations centered around Christ. I felt a spiritual bond with him, and yet he was gently romantic. I felt like a lady. And I couldn't help but think that he might be the knight I'd been praying for.

Then in April he asked me if I wanted to go with him and several others to Dayton to hear Kathryn Kuhlman. Four springs had passed since I had been to her meeting in Chicago.

What better time? What better place? Under whose blessed ministry could my healing better be manifested? In the six years since the accident, I had learned the definition of patience, of waiting on the Lord. Surely now would be my time for "walking and leaping and praising God" (Acts 3:8). Images of being with Mike, being cloaked in the robe of healing, were imprinted in my mind.

The Dayton Convention Center was full. After waiting over an hour for the doors to open, we were finally seated fifteen rows from the main floor, directly across from the choir. We waited another half hour before Miss Kuhlman came to the platform.

Mike and I talked little as we watched the people fill the seats all the way to the high balcony. I had noticed coming down the aisle that it had no railing; Mike's elbow had been the railing I needed. I knew that the only way I could go down to the auditorium floor by myself was to have perfect balance—to be completely healed.

But would it happen? I thought about the meeting in Chicago. I knew the power of God worked through her. I had seen miracles in her Chicago meeting. I knew I could be one of them. It wasn't my turn then; I hoped it would be now.

She entered in white, in grace, in slender beauty. She was just as I had remembered her. Long, sheer sleeves extended from her gown, floating as she moved, giving her an angelic appearance. Her words penetrated my expectations. While she spoke, I didn't look at anyone but her. My eyes and heart were shadows of her movements.

"Will you please stand," she said as the meeting came to a close. Pushing from both armrests, I stood, my hands resting on the seat in front for balance.

"God wants to work miracles in you here today. His love is

great. He loves you," she continued, drawing out the word *love,* drawing us in with it. "He wants to touch you."

Pausing, she raised both hands. Her sleeves looked like an angel's wings. "Oh, isn't God wonderful?" Her smile was her affirmation. She pronounced the name of *God* with awe, with a hint of British accent, the *d* sounding like a *t.* With every word, her slow drawl stretched and emphasized her sentences.

The audience responded to her love invitation. From various sections of the auditorium men, women, teenagers, and children filtered down to the gym floor, crowding around the platform. One after the other, testimonies of healings and miracles were given. There was weeping and praising. Kathryn proclaimed again and again, her slender frame leaning toward the microphone, "Isn't God wonderful?"

I listened, nodding a yes to her question. I praised God for being God and closed my eyes, waiting. My heart was on its knees as I waited to feel the glorious change, the freeing of my body from its prison of paralysis.

Soon I could hear the quieting of the auditorium. An urgency wound its way through me, a desperation. I didn't want to open my eyes. The meeting was closing, and I was still untouched: no electrical surge, no oil warmth, no intense heat. I peered at Mike with one eye. He was firm, eyes locked to Kathryn. Cries and pleas churned inside, promises of faithfulness and dedication were underscored by my tears. *Lord, please, heal me. I'm ready. I'm waiting. Touch me, Lord. I believe in You.*

The choir sang the final song. Kathryn drifted offstage just as she had entered, with hands raised, with a smiling benediction, "God bless you. God bless you." Around me people sighed, emotionally spent. Then they turned, gathered coats and jackets, and moved into the aisles to begin their exit.

I was too numb to sigh. My mind had no thoughts; my body had no feelings. I refused to think about what had not happened. I barred the doors and windows of my mind and turned the key, imprisoning my brain.

Mike handed me my jacket and escorted me up the long flight of stairs. We were silent, milling with the crowd.

"I think I'll go to the ladies' room before we leave. I saw one at the top of these stairs when we were coming in." My voice sounded far away, echoing from my prison walls.

"Okay. I'll meet with the others, and we'll pull the van to that door." He pointed to the one just beyond the ladies' room.

"Fine. I'll meet you there."

He turned to the left toward the front entrance, while I went straight ahead. Cordially, I greeted several women going in, thanking one for holding the door open for me. But, it wasn't me; it was an image of me. I was locked away.

On the way back to Muncie, everyone talked about the presence of God during the meeting—the miracles, the healings, the lumps which had dissolved, the eyes which had seen, the pain and stiffness which had disappeared. I affirmed this presence: God had moved. I had seen it and I couldn't deny it. Not that I wanted to deny it, but I had wanted Him to move in me. My face smiled, my voice laughed. I was hot inside and out. Removing my jacket cooled my outer body temperature, but I couldn't remove the heat on the inside. I was a tense battleground. In words and actions, I treaded with caution, tiptoeing, lest a faulty step explode a land mine. The hurt burned in my heart.

Good-byes and thank yous were exchanged when Mike and I got out of the van at his house.

"Get in my folks' car, Jama. I'll get the keys and say hello to Mom. Be right back." He sprinted to the porch and into the house. He was back almost before the screen door he had gone through slammed shut. I was just swinging my legs into the car. Shutting the door for me, he went around to the driver's side.

We had left at seven that morning, and I was tired after the long day and desperately needed understanding and compassion. I didn't want Mike to take me directly to the dorm. I hoped he might take me for a drive or a Coke. I needed someone to tell me that there was nothing wrong with my heart or my faith that was preventing my healing. But I was afraid to reach out to him, afraid to reveal all the pain I had swirling within, the whirlpool force that was pulling me under. I waited to see if he would know my hurt.

As he drove through campus, I knew he was taking me directly to Botsford. I said nothing when he opened the car door for me. There was a silence, a sense of strain.

"Thanks for going with me." He was too cordial, but I knew he was sincere. I felt as if I had disappointed him because there had been no miracle in my body. I pushed the disappointment behind a smile.

"Thanks for asking me." I felt awkward, fidgeting with my purse strap. "See you later," I added, trying to make it sound like a statement rather than a question. He was around the car, ready to open the door.

"Take it easy!" he said and stepped back into the car.

"Thanks!" My smile was feeble. I raised my arm in a good-bye wave as he drove away. More sadness rolled in. I had needed his hug, or some affectionate contact. He had always kissed me good-bye before.

As I walked into the hall, I wondered what he was thinking. We had never talked about the question of my healing, but I thought that he, too, had expected something to happen in Dayton. Being schooled in faith teachings, we both had the same eyes of trust and saw beyond the crutch. But did he think that I lacked faith? That it was some lack in me that was the cause of no visual change? I knew that God was powerful and a keeper of promises. And yet, as I slowly moved my body into the dorm, my faith groped in a fog of doubts, and I tried to understand the timing of God's promises.

I moved my feet, the crutch, my feet, the crutch, mechanically, past the lounge, past the reception desk, past the mailboxes, through the double doors, down the hallway, and into my room. I locked the door. Denise was gone for the weekend as were many others. It was seven o'clock, and the halls were unusually quiet, but nothing was quiet within me. I sat on the edge of the bed. My heart erupted, the land mine of emotions blew, my protective walls shattered.

I had no power to suppress the tears. I had no strength to quiet the sobs. I crumbled on the bed, turning my face into the pillow to muffle the cries. My body shook uncontrollably; I had never wept with such intensity or passion. The "why" crashed down hard upon my vulnerability.

*Why didn't You heal me today? I was ready, I was ready.
Haven't I waited long enough? I was expectant. I believed. I did
everything I knew how to do. Why? Why? Why didn't You do it?
I'm Your child. You love me. Don't You want the very best thing
for me? Don't You think that healing me would be the best thing?
Don't You know how much more glory You would receive?*

I questioned. I pouted. I was stretched over a dark abyss, and
I didn't know if I could hang on. My fingers hurt from clinging.
I was ready to let go.

But I was being supported by a power much stronger than my
own humanity. The well of tears dried and I cleared a throat that
was sore from the wretched sobs. I struggled to sit up. The ache
in my fingers lessened. I would not let go of God's promises. I
knew that if I did I would die. I would be denying God, and I
could not live without Him. How could I turn my back on God
when I knew that my source of life was in Him, that He had saved
me from death? I had to believe that I was in His plan, believe and
not question so much.

Think positively, Jama, don't cry.

Two tissues dried my face and eyes. I blew my nose. Crying
was not going to explain anything to me. I could not cry my way
into a healing. I got up and called Mom. I knew that she too had
been believing that I would come home and run up to the house
to hug her hello. I told her about all the healings, all surface
talk. I didn't mention what my heart had gone through or what
it was still going through. It was too hard to put my jumbled
emotions into words.

Mom knew my disappointment; she knew my hurt. She wanted
to get in the car and drive over to comfort me, but she also knew
that this time I had to rely on the Spirit for pure comfort, and only
the Spirit. She held back her own tears for me as she thought about
the long wait. The pain was much deeper than I could explain.
Even Mom didn't know how deep it was or how precariously I was
balanced. Only God's grace was keeping me from a fall into total
rejection and denial of my very faith in Him.

"We'll pick you up for church in the morning, okay?" Her voice
was soft with love and emotion.

"Okay."

"Are you all right, sweetheart? You want to come home for the night?"

"No, I'm okay. I'm just tired and worn out from everything. I don't feel like moving."

"Well, if you're sure . . . we'll see you about nine." Then she added as if knowing how much I needed to hear it, "I love you."

The tears nearly erupted again. "Thanks, Mom. I love you, too."

After I hung up the phone, I wanted to be alone, yet I also needed to hear voices, some words of comfort. I put Denise's three Christian albums on her record player and lay back down on the bed. I felt the music embrace me like a warm blanket, covering my vulnerability and the shattered pieces of my emotions. I was letting God recreate what the hurt had exploded. But this time, He was not allowing me to create my own walls around my inner being. Instead of the prison of pain, this time He would build a mansion of peace for me. He was the Foundation.

Exhaustion enveloped me as the music floated in the air. The Spirit was speaking comforting promises to my heart that I could not forget. *I will never leave you nor forsake you . . . Lean not unto thine own understanding. . . . My ways are not thy ways. . . . Believe in me and thou shalt be saved. . . . Fret not thyself. . . . I have come that you might have joy. . . . But my God shall supply all thy needs according to his riches in glory by Christ Jesus. . . . I shall give thee the desires of thine heart. . . . Wait thou upon God. . . .*

I repented. I apologized and wept again in conviction. I gave up fighting to understand.

Father, I prayed. *I can't do it. I feel alone and I don't understand. Comfort me, love me. Send me angels. I'm Yours and I want to know that I'm in Your will. I want to have patience, but I'm so weak. But I love You and believe You and I'm sorry.*

The tears had washed away the bitterness and the pain. My prayer had taken me beyond the disappointment and the defeat I had felt only hours before. God was indeed building my mansion of peace. I felt supernatural comfort, but I felt even more: My comfort was God Himself. Healing was in my heart.

15

The Source of Strength and Creativity

"I feel pretty strong today," I said.

"Think you want to try some more?"

"Sure. I think I can handle it."

Tim, the therapist at the Ball State Health Center, removed the pin from the 150-pound slot and inserted it into the next slot.

"Okay. Let's see your stuff," he said.

I adjusted my feet on the leg press, gripped the metal bars on the seat, and pushed with everything I had. Groan. The first one was always the hardest; but then, once the weights were up, the repetitions were easier. I watched the weights go up and down as I bent my legs, feeling the strain of muscles in my thighs; my hands hurt from the tight grip.

I counted: *one, two, three, four, five, six.* But as I tried for seven, the weights crashed against each other as I relaxed my legs.

I was out of breath; my heart raced. One hundred and eighty pounds. Eighty pounds over my own body weight!

"Good job!" Tim said, his eyes sparkling. "Take a rest."

I had been going down to the physical therapy department in the Health Center since the second quarter of my freshman year. I received credit for the six physical education requirements because of Ball State's Adapted Physical Education program. But long after I had met the requirements, I continued to go twice a week.

When I first began the therapy, Tim helped me lift weights with my arms and legs and do range-of-motion exercises. I could hardly lift two and a half pounds in the bench press position, and with each leg I could press only ten pounds.

Gradually, I began lifting more weight with my arms, and I increased the leg weight to 60 pounds. When the department purchased a universal weight-lifting machine, I began lifting 40 pounds on the bench press and the military press. And because of the machine, I could leg press the weights with both legs instead of each leg independently. Now, three years later, my strength had increased, and I had reached my top weight of pressing 180 with both legs. The soreness in my muscles from working with the weights, doing the exercises, riding the stationary bike wasn't pain to me: It was wonderful, glorious strength.

My accomplishments in therapy were an example of how far I had come physically, as well as my increased spiritual and emotional strength. After the struggles and pain of my freshman year, the Lord sent two years of pleasant sailing as a sophomore and junior. There were no storms, no tempestuous questionings. He sent me more Christian friends, especially a blessed, new roommate named Joanne. My friendship with her became one of the greatest blessings that God has given me.

I let God dissolve the hurt in my heart when Mike never asked me out again after the trip to Dayton. God comforted me and I purposed in my heart that I could still be desirable as a woman even while walking with the crutch. I learned that I couldn't dwell on what I didn't have, I had to make that leap of faith and trust God even more concerning my relationships with males. In His faithfulness, God brought several male friends into my company. It was fun to joke and be pals with many of the guys who lived in Swinford, Botsford's brother dorm. One guy especially, Rod, showed a romantic interest in me that caused my self-image to rise. He was an English major too and at times acted comically insane, yet he had a sensitivity that made me feel very feminine and desirable.

For a while my life was smooth sailing; security and comfort filled my sails. The question of my postponed healing was still aboard, but it was boxed and stored in a lower cabin. God didn't have to explain Himself to me. I loved Him; I trusted Him; I waited on Him.

The three years of living in the dorm seemed to draw me closer to my family. The separation made me take them less for granted as is often common. I knew that I was growing up, maturing, but I wasn't growing away from them as much as I was growing toward them, in a healthy interdependence and not isolation.

I felt the intensity of my love for each of them burn more deeply. I counted the quarter breaks and summers as precious because I could be at home. I enjoyed every moment and didn't want to waste it by bickering with Steve, Doug, and Julee about small things: which TV show to watch, who should use the car, who should load the dishwasher—all the typical brother-sister squabbles. In my desire to get along and to enjoy everyone for the short time I would be home, I didn't mind doing the dishes or watching what they wanted.

There were now three of us at Ball State; however, I was the only one living away from home. Steve and Doug were not embarrassed by their sister who rode the ponderous bike around campus. They never ignored me or looked the other way when they saw me coming. In fact, they were proud of me for my perseverance —an attitude they had had since high school. They had no hangups because I was different. I was their sister, and the accident had altered very little the way in which they treated me. They still teased me and argued with me, but when they knew I needed them, they were there. That first year after my accident, when my bladder muscles had been so weak and Mom had yelled, "Boys!" one or both had always come running, picked me up, and carried me to the bathroom. They didn't complain, because they knew that at that point I needed their help.

Once Steve told me that he had overheard a guy talking to a girl in one of his classes about this girl he had seen who rode a big tricycle and walked with a crutch. Steve turned around in his seat and smiled, "Hey, that's my sister."

"She sure can pump that bike. I've seen her when it's been pouring down rain." The guy smiled.

"Yes, she's living in the dorm." He chuckled. "You know, it's kind of ironic. My brother and I are living at home and going to Ball State, and my sister is living away. You'd think it'd be the other way around. She's something else." Like Dad, Steve was never one to think that there was anything I couldn't do.

The winter vacation of 1976 brought several inches of snow to the midwest; we all delighted in the white Christmas. A few days after the holiday, about nine o'clock one evening, light flakes started to fall again. Dad had built a fire, and we were in the living room watching television and enjoying the warmth. Suddenly, Steve decided that he wanted to go sledding.

"Sledding? At this hour?" Mom had questioned.

"Come on, you guys," he coaxed. "We can call a bunch of friends, and nobody should be on the hills at this time of night. It'll be fun."

Steve had always been the entertainment chairman of the family. Doug and Julee thought it was a great idea. I felt a bubble of self-pity start to rise when suddenly it was popped.

"Okay, great. And Jama, you're going, too. I think you can go down on a sled so you better bundle up."

Excitedly, Mom helped me pull on three pairs of socks, two pairs of pants, two sweaters, and a sweatshirt. I could hardly move. Steve busily called as many friends as he could think of who were also home for the vacation. He told them to come to our house and then we would squeeze into two or three cars and head for McCullough Park. By the time everyone came it was after ten-thirty.

We didn't find out how cold it had been while we were sledding until the next day: eight degrees below zero. No wonder I was so cold as I stood by one of the cars and watched everyone sled. We didn't have enough sleds for everyone, so many of us were huddled together by the car. A few who hadn't dressed warmly enough sat inside the car. Someone had brought a large piece of plastic and as many as ten could sit on it and slide partway down the hill before toppling in the snow.

We must have been at the park for almost an hour when the

cold night air pierced through our clothing and made most of us ready to head back to our house for hot chocolate. Just as I was turning to get into the car, Steve yelled, "Wait a minute! Jama, you haven't gone down yet!" He sprinted toward me with a red sled.

"Steve, that's okay. I'm so cold I can hardly move. I just like watching." The sled looked so little, and the two trees at the bottom of the hill looked so big.

"No. Now you came along and you have to go down at least once; what's the fun of sledding if you don't sled? Come on guys, let's grab her!"

"Yikes!" I screeched as I was grabbed and placed on the sled. Steve then lay down on top of me. My mittened hands held the steering lever as tightly as they could.

"Now you just let me do the steering. There are a couple of rough bumps I don't want to hit," he said. "I'll try not to squish you."

"Thanks. And don't hit the trees either, okay?" Excitement and fear tumbled inside me.

"Haven't hit them so far. Hey, someone give us a push!"

The laughter from the top of the hill faded as we bounced down the hill, and the sound of the metal runners on the frozen snow filled my ears. I don't know if the screams inside me came out of my mouth or not. Cold air burned my cheeks, and I wanted to close my eyes but they wouldn't blink. Whiteness was everywhere and the trees grew larger. Steve turned the steering lever sharply as we bumped toward the bottom. As he did so, I lost my grip, and we both rolled onto the hard snow. Laughter erupted from the top and lying there covered with cold snow, we laughed too. I was on my back looking directly into the huge naked branches of a tree. My heart raced, and pleasure filled me completely.

Steve yelled for Gary who came running, and together they carried me back up the hill, slowly because the snow was one slick surface.

The cold had stiffened my body, and I could barely walk into the house. It was after midnight when we got home, and we all thawed in front of the fire. The warmth went through me because my enjoyment of the evening had not been vicarious but actual. I wanted to thank Steve. I would never have thought that I could go down on the sled had he not suggested it and followed through.

For the most part, my family never considered me too weak or too fragile to try new things. When we went to the King's Island Amusement Park, I rode the same rides as everyone, except for the big roller coasters. The sight of them scared me silly, let alone the thought of being on one. And later, on my twenty-second birthday, our family went horseback riding down on the hilly trails of southern Indiana. I rode double with the trail guide, but I did ride the biggest horse in the stables: Big Red.

During vacations at home, I began to take another step—walking without the crutch. The steps were childlike, tottering, but they were steps, and I was taking them *alone.* My family, especially Steve and Dad, saw the necessity in my practicing walking as much as possible. The pattern was still there: a step of faith, practice, exercise, improvement, strength. Frustration and tears were always interwoven into that pattern.

During my spring quarter break in 1977, Mom and Dad went on their second trip to the Holy Land as tour hosts with George Otis, a friend and Christian writer and publisher from the west coast. As substitute father figure while Mom and Dad were gone, Steve decided that I should leave the crutch by the kitchen door and use it only when I had to go out. He gave me this information the day after the folks had left. This seemed like a good idea until one evening when Steve brought home Mary, a girl he had met at the Christian coffeehouse downtown. Mary and I would later become close friends and roommates. On that night, however, I didn't want her to see my instability when I walked without a crutch.

We were all sitting in the living room by the fire, watching TV. Thinking that Steve and Mary might want to be alone, I put the magazine I was reading on the floor beside my chair, then reached for the crutch I had laid there.

"Night you two." I said, using the crutch and the armrest as supports to push up from the chair.

"Good-night, Jama." Mary's voice was sweet.

"Jama, I thought you were going to leave the crutch at the doorway in the kitchen this whole week while you're home. How come you're using it now?" Steve asked.

I didn't answer directly, but mumbled an "I know." I hadn't forgotten, but using it was so much easier, and with Mary there I didn't want to be embarrassed by falling down. Steve was right and I knew it, but I felt defensive. "Just quit bugging me," I wanted to tell him, "you don't know how hard and frustrating it is."

When I walked without the crutch, my steps were tiny and halting as I concentrated totally on maintaining balance. Sometimes I thought that I was walking backward instead of forward because I moved so slowly.

Lying in bed that night, I felt ashamed of being impolite to Steve and Mary. When Steve had confronted me with not using the crutch, I had turned cold, and whether or not they sensed the difference, I knew what I was feeling inside, and it was wrong. I had left the room silently after a short, "Night." With closed eyes, I apologized to the Lord for my negative attitude and determined that no matter how frustrated I got, I *would* leave the crutch at the doorway. Frustration did come, and at times I fought back the tears. But by the end of the week, I didn't fear falling so much. As time passed, I felt more confident about leaving the crutch and walking alone. It has since become a habit, and now I always leave the crutch leaning on the wall by the door as soon as I enter.

After three years of living in Botsford, I was ready for a change. I knew that I had only one more quarter before early graduation, and I wanted to try apartment living. That summer of 1977 I lived at home until August, and then I moved into a two-bedroom house a few blocks from campus. Three other girls would live with me: Mary was already there; Joanne and another friend, Chris, would move in with us as soon as school began in September.

Life in the beginning of the summer was sunshine and laughter and gentle times with Mary as we became closer friends. But as autumn neared, the moments became dark and painful. My approaching graduation in mid-November had aroused my doubts. All the apprehension and fear about leaving my comfortable world, the same emotions I had had during my senior year in high school, came flooding back. Again, I wanted the question of my healing to be answered, to be completed.

Lord, who would want to hire me the way I am now? Why not finish the healing so I won't have to worry about that?"

I knew that if I was not freed from my tight cocoon of questions and impatience I would decay. The summer was a change, a resurrection. The more I allowed God to work the change, the more strength I had in destroying the doubt and selfishness. He had led me, and He would continue to lead me if I put my hand in His. He was there in rest and quiet and waiting, that I might learn obedience and enter, too, into that rest and quiet and waiting.

But all too often, my waiting was more of a struggle than a rest. A major part of that struggling was the battle that had started when I had decided to leave the crutch by the door whenever I was indoors. At my parents' and especially at the apartment, I heard a war horn and knew a battle was beginning. It was at the apartment, where I was often alone, that I battled between persistence and surrender, between lethargy and tenacity, between frustration and tranquility. Countless times I wanted to head for the door to retrieve that crutch, that material support, that easy way out. Swords of thought clashed yes, no, fight, yield. My mind was the battlefield.

One summer night after I had said good-night to Mary and had gone to my bedroom, I saw a slip of paper leaning against the jewelry box when I turned on the light. I recognized Mary's handwriting.

Jama,
　　What do you feel when I suggest that you not use the crutch? Do you feel, "She can't understand what I go through?" Or what?
　　You just say, "I know" But what do you know?
　　I want to share with you your feelings, fears, and hurts,
　　so that we can bring them to the Lord together as a body.

I love you in His love,
Mary

I lay on my bed in the silent darkness and wept.

"Jama?" Her voice was tenderly quiet that next evening when she came home from work and saw me working on some poetry manuscripts to send out. "Jama, did you see the note I left in your bedroom last night?" She sat down on the edge of the couch and looked into my eyes.

I sighed and fought back the tears as I saw the compassion in her face.

"Yes, I saw it," I nodded.

"And?" she encouraged.

Mentally formulating what I wanted to say, I sighed again and turned sideways in the desk chair to face her. The words began to tumble out.

"Mary, I say, 'I know' when you ask me about not using the crutch because I *know* I should be walking more and more by myself so that my balance will improve. But it seems like I've done that so many times and not seen any real progress, so I tend to slide back into using it again. I get aggravated with myself when I use the crutch, but when I walk alone, I walk so much slower and I have to concentrate to keep my balance. There is also a greater chance that I'll fall. I don't know, Mary. I just get tired of working at it all the time. So, I keep using the crutch." I paused and looked into her face. I wasn't sure what to say next.

Kneeling down in front of my chair, she took my hands. A volcano of tears was rising to the surface from deep within me and I sighed again to release the pressure.

"Jama, do you think God's going to instantaneously heal you?" She spoke the words my heart had asked many times.

"Mary," I held my friend's warm hands, "for a long time I thought that would be how God would complete my healing—instantaneously. All along it's been a gradual thing, first one accomplishment and then another. I've had to walk every step of the healing. And I do mean *walk*. If I had had a choice, I probably wouldn't have chosen this way. But in my heart I know that God has been molding my character and making me a stronger person and a better witness for Him. I know He wants to finish what He began. It's sure hard to wait but I'm going to always hang onto the vision I have of being totally healed." My smile was weak, but our eyes held contact.

"Jama, I really think that God wants you to work harder on your walking. I don't think that He wants you to sit around and wait for the miracle to happen. Walk out the healing that He has already given you. Not that you can heal yourself, but don't use the crutch, especially around the apartment. Use the muscles that God brought back to you. I'll help you if you fall, and you shouldn't be embarrassed. If I'm not here, He'll help you." Her quiet voice was firm. My volcano erupted. The tears fell hot and burning on my cheeks.

She continued, "You'll probably say that I don't know what it's like for you. And I guess that's true. But you don't have to struggle through it alone, Jama. We're supposed to bear each other's burdens." I saw small tears creep from her eyes. "You've got the greatest strength in the universe to lean on, and you've got me, too."

As the truth of Mary's words hit me, I could find no answers. My mind became a projection screen. Scenes of hurts and frustrations and disappointments flashed by, scenes of my slow, laborious walk, my falling, my unextending fingers. I wanted this grim moving picture to halt. I was tired of the struggling, the thinking, the waiting.

"Practice your walking! Exercise for God's glory!" Mary said, reaching up and hugging me. We both cried, our emotions spanning our communication.

And I did practice. Once again I came to the grand revelation of God's Almighty Presence—everywhere. Although I felt secure at school, the fear of graduation began to diminish. I realized that God had always taken care of me before, no matter what my physical condition, and He would certainly be with me in the future. Through His grace, I knew that wherever I went, God would go before me. When I stumbled and felt myself losing balance, "Jesus" was the word I uttered. He was on my left hand and on my right; He was before me and behind me. In His hands I felt protected.

As soon as I made the vow not to fear falling, I fell. I had never been hurt physically, since I had learned how to roll with the fall, but there was the psychological hurt, the helplessness. But I was also learning that I could tap into the Source of Creativity, that I could pray for His creativeness to inspire me, to show me how I could get out of struggling situations.

After church one Sunday, I had gone over to my folks' house to visit with everyone. We had all laughed and joked and watched TV, and before I knew it, it was after eleven o'clock. Before I left to go back to the apartment, Doug gave me a record album as a late birthday present. He even took it out to the car for me. Dad and I had come to an agreement about the specially equipped Duster, our second car: It would be partly an early graduation present and partly purchased with my own savings.

Parking the car in the gravel by the side of the house, I noticed that the lights were all out, which meant no one else was home. The only light came from the streetlight on the corner. As I was getting out, trying to manipulate the album, my purse, and the crutch, I slipped on the dewy grass and fell. "Jesus," I gasped as I saw the distance between my face and the ground close in. I turned as I hit and rolled onto the wet grass.

Whenever I had fallen before, God had always been faithful to have someone come along to help me up, or to have a couch or chair close enough so that I could push myself up. But tonight no one was home and the streets were empty. I was sprawled out on the lawn in the midnight darkness. As tears welled up, I checked myself and went over my options.

Now, Jama, you can do one of three things: You can just sit yourself up and cry, which will sap all your strength so that even if you could get up you'd be too tired. Or you can yell for help, but probably no one will hear you since you're parked on this side street. Or you can pray and ask God how in the world He's going to get you out of this one.

I opted for the latter.

I sat up and put the crutch, purse, and album back in the car on the floor behind the driver's seat. Then I scooted my body backward so I was leaning against the car. I thought about how I used to get up onto our living room couch. I had to push my back all the way against it, then reach back with my hands to get leverage on the cushions. With my knees bent to my chest, I had to force down with my arm muscles until I got about halfway up. Then, pushing with my leg muscles, I could raise my bottom onto the cushions. I tried this same procedure to get back into the car, but it didn't work because the driver's seat was too high.

Okay, Lord, I wondered, *now what?*

I twisted my body around so that I was kneeling, eye level with the car seat. "Perfect praying position," I chuckled and sighed. Since I couldn't get into the car backward, maybe I could go in forward. What if I pushed with my legs and pulled on the steering wheel? Maybe, just maybe, I could slide into the car on my stomach.

Gritting my teeth and uttering a desperate prayer for strength, I grabbed the steering wheel with my left hand and pushed against the seat with my right. Again and again, my feet slid on the wet grass and gravel, and I coached the Lord and myself. *C'mon, c'mon, push those legs, PUSH!* I kept pushing with my feet and pulling on the steering wheel. "Jesus, Jesus, Jesus," I groaned.

Finally I felt my feet leave the ground, and I wiggled and wormed and pulled on the wheel until I could feel my pelvic bones against the car seat. In the next moment, I was lying all the way across the seat on my stomach, my head six inches from the other door. I rolled over on my back and closed my eyes.

"Oh, Lord," I whispered. "Thank You, thank You." I was so exhausted I felt like sleeping right where I was. But I pulled on the steering wheel to help me sit up, and I sat and praised God. I was tempted to toot the horn, I was so thrilled that once again He had given me strength to do the impossible. He would never leave me. He was with me. I was at peace in His endless love for me.

"Oh, God," I smiled and shouted into the night sky, "I love You!"

16

The Latter End

Out of the corner of my eye, I watched Joanne as she sat cross-legged on the couch, meticulously trimming the edges on the magazine figures that she had cut out for another student teaching lesson plan. Whether she knew I was glancing at her and was ignoring the natural impulse to look up when stared at, or whether she was that involved in removing the excess edge, I couldn't tell. Every time I turned my head back toward my textbook lying open on the desk, my eyes fell on the same lines I had already read six times. I read them for the seventh, then lifted my eyes, forgetting the lines again as I stared into the blank white wall, and thought about my friendship with Joanne.

We had met in our freshman year when we had lived three rooms apart. Almost every night we had brushed our teeth at the same time. And, after a few weeks being that "intimate," we began talking more and more when we'd see each other outside the bathroom. Since her room was the first one in the hall, I often stopped and talked to her on the way to my room, two doors down. Then one night after we had rinsed the Crest from our mouths, and she had dropped her toothbrush into her yellow Shedd's Peanut Butter bucket, I looked at her, pulled up courage, gulped, and asked, "Joanne, how would you like to be roommates next year." I was afraid to wait for her answer, afraid she would say no so I babbled, "I know that Cindi isn't coming back to school, and Denise isn't either I don't think, and I thought that maybe it would be better to ask someone I knew to be roommates than to go potluck again or whatever. What do you think?"

"I think you talk awfully fast." She laughed, a laugh that melted that cold wall of fear, the old fear of rejection. She swung her towel around her shoulder, grabbed her bucket, and opened the bathroom door. I followed her out, grabbing my bucket from the sink counter.

"I had a feeling that you were going to ask me that. Cindi told me that you talked to her." She smiled and leaned against the wall between the bathroom door and the door to Denise's and my room. I wanted her to just say yes, but she kept hinting. "Cindi said that you would probably be asking me something pretty soon. I guess I kind of knew what it was going to be about."

She smiled. I knew that the smile was saying yes, but I wanted her to say it for confirmation. She did. "Yes, I think we could get along pretty well as roommates." The rest of what we talked about there in the hallway that night was blurred by the fact that she had said yes. I remember her laugh as she tilted her head back against the wall, her hair on top of her head, bun fashion with four spongy, pink rollers. I remember how she swung her bucket as she talked about her boyfriend, and the coincidence that my Aunt Billie in Fort Wayne knew her boyfriend's mother. Talking and laughing, we spent more than an hour sharing about our families, our classes, and whatever else came to mind. I remember thinking, as I headed for my door and she toward her room, that we might never get a full night's sleep when we were roommates if we were always going to talk so much.

And we always did seem to talk a lot. For the next two years we were roommates, and with each year my love for Joanne and the value of our friendship multiplied. We talked about everything —our dreams of being married to wonderful Christian guys, her dream of being a teacher of the deaf, my dream of writing poetry and Christian literature. We talked about the difficulty of being Christians and keeping our heads when all those around seemed to be losing theirs.

Gradually, we began to share what we were learning in our "quiet times" and our Bible readings. I felt no embarrassment in saying on my way to class as I loaded my satchel with the books I needed, "Joanne, I'm a little nervous about taking this test; would you pray for me at one when I'm taking it?" And likewise, she asked me to pray about her exams or her problems with her boyfriend. Our relationship grew to the point where I thought that we could talk about anything. And I always wanted to talk to Joanne. I wanted to know what she thought about everything.

In the two years of living in that small dorm room, I thought that the Lord had really blessed us in that we hardly ever argued or disagreed. I was always conscious of trying to be the best friend and roommate that I could. I knew that living with me was difficult at times because of my physical limitations, and I tried to compensate by doing Joanne favors like proofreading her term papers or typing them. Her friendship was so important to me that I wanted to do anything I could to help her. It was my way of thanking her for being a friend to me. I had never had a friend like her before, and I didn't want to do anything to lose her love or friendship.

But now, something was wrong, very wrong. Mary and I had moved into the apartment in August. Joanne and Chris had arrived in September, And for a while everything had gone smoothly. Mary had already graduated from college in Missouri and had taken a job as a marketing director for the Muncie Mall. Her job kept her busy, and since her schedule was erratic, she wasn't in the apartment much. Chris also had a job, as a photographer, which kept her running here and there. Joanne was busy with her education projects and preparing for student teaching during the winter. I went to classes in the mornings and worked afternoons at Mom's gift store.

Since we weren't in the apartment together very often, I wasn't sure when the tension started to build, but it did. Here we were in mid-October and there was a barrier between each of us, especially between me and Joanne. There was a silence that I had never felt before. No one was really talking to anyone. No one was communicating the love of the Lord—no one, including me. The more the other three girls kept silent, the more I closed up, fearing that I was the cause.

As Joanne kept working on her lesson plan, my eyes began to hurt from staring at my book and then at the wall. My heart ached as I thought about what was happening to our friendship. Living in the apartment together had seemed like such a good idea, especially since we were all Christians. But now the silence mocked us all. A few more minutes went by, and still the only sound was the snip-snip of Joanne's scissors. Finally I knew the problem had to be attacked head-on. I turned from the desk to face Joanne on the couch.

"Joanne, please talk to me." My voice was quiet for two reasons: Chris and Mary were sleeping in the bedroom just off the living room, and for the first time in our friendship, I was uncomfortable being with Joanne. Uneasiness sometimes displays itself in soft voices.

"Please, Joanne, something's wrong, and I can't take this silence and tension any more. I can't concentrate on my studies and I can't sleep very well because I'm thinking that I've done something around here to upset everyone. If I have, please tell me so that I can correct whatever it is. But, please, don't give me the silent treatment. I can't take it."

My voice grew stronger with each sentence. I focused my eyes on her face but she looked away. I didn't know what else to say.

"I should really keep working on this project, Jama. It's due tomorrow." Her words were choppy with uneasiness. Her scissors snipped away the paper with greater speed.

I fought to control the whine in my voice and to force down the lump in my throat. "Joanne, please. Talk to me. Tell me what's going on. Why is everyone acting so strange? Why are there no smiles or any laughing in the house anymore? And what's the matter with you and me? When I come into a room, you leave. Or when I'm in one room, you pass through it to be in another room. I ask you a question and you hardly talk to me. Joanne, I need to understand. Please tell me what you're thinking."

The whine crept into my last few words. My body was numb on the desk chair as I waited for her response. Laying the scissors down, she scooted back against the couch, and pulled her legs under her Indian-style, then wrapped her arms around her waist and looked at me. Her look was very serious—almost grim.

"I'm not sure where to begin, but you're right, there's a lot of tension in this house. It's so much different than I thought it was going to be and so much different than the dorm. I don't think everything's your fault but things seem to have multiplied. I see what everyone else does around here and then what you *don't* do. I guess I resent that you don't seem to do your share, and that I have to do it for you. Then I start feeling guilty because of your accident, which only makes the resentment build, because I don't want to feel guilty and I resent you for making me feel that way. When Chris or Mary ask me to do something for them, I don't think anything of it. But when you ask me to do the same thing, resentment pours in. I think that you should do it for yourself. I know I'm probably wrong, but I can't help the way I've been feeling. It's been building up for a long time."

"It seems like I can't win either way." My voice was a hurt whisper.

"Jama, remember we talked about this in the dorm one night last spring. You asked me if I was ever put out because of the times I did things for you. I was honest with you then and told you that it really bothered me when you would hint around about wanting something without coming right out and asking."

"Yes, but you weren't specific. What bothers you?"

"It's just that you assume so much. Okay, like the wastebaskets for example. That may seem trivial, but it did bother me. You would never ask me to empty it. You would just assume that when I emptied mine, I would see that yours needed it too and do it for you. I know that the trash bin was down the hall and getting to it with the wastebasket would be hard, but it was the fact that you wouldn't ask me—that's what bothered me. Everything would be going great with us; we'd be laughing and having fun, but then all the responsibility that I felt because I had to do double everything —once for me and once for you—would mount up and I would feel terrible. Then what made it worse was that I felt so unchristian because of my bad thoughts. Here I was healthy and you had been through so much that I shouldn't mind doing things for you even if you didn't ask. But I did mind. It would have been better if you had asked me.

"And you do the same thing now. I feel it especially because I've lived with you longer, but I think Mary and Chris feel it too."

Her sentences jabbed at my tender vulnerability and at the old insecurity about being different. I didn't know what to say.

"I didn't know you felt that way. Why didn't you tell me before? You've been carrying that around all this time?"

"I didn't tell you because I felt so bad about those feelings. I wanted so badly for them to change, but they've only gotten worse."

"But if it bothered you . . . I'm sorry."

"Now you're making me feel even guiltier."

"Well, my gosh, Joanne, I don't know what to do. How am I supposed to feel?" A touch of anger came through, and I pulled up my defenses. "If you didn't tell me, how was I supposed to know that emptying the wastebaskets bothered you?" I was too afraid to ask her if everything she had done for me in the last two years had bothered her.

"No, you don't understand. It wasn't just the wastebaskets. That's just an example. It's just that it seems you assume so much. If I emptied my wastebasket, you'd assume I'd empty yours. If I'd get a drink, I'd get one for you. I want to help you, but it has just gotten to be more than I can handle. Now I feel like I'm not my own person."

"But you just said that even if I were to ask, you would feel resentment toward me."

"I guess I've let everything build up to that point. I know I probably should have told you then, when it happened, but I just couldn't. You see, I felt I was wrong for having those feelings. I felt so guilty. No one understood and no one else seemed to feel the way I did—not your other friends or your family. That's why I couldn't say anything. But now, though I still feel bad about it Jama, I knew I had to tell you."

"Okay. I'm sorry. I know I shouldn't say that—you'll feel guilty. But I *am* sorry. I had no idea you'd been holding all this stuff in. It's really been eating away at you. I don't know what to do. What's going to happen to us, to our friendship? Or don't you consider me your friend any more?"

"Of course you are my friend." Her voice was quiet. "I just need time to get over these feelings."

Silence filled the room, crowding against me so that Joanne seemed far away. We couldn't look at each other. I felt an urgency to leave the room. The hurt billowed inside. Joanne picked up the scissors and began her careful trimming. I closed my book and got up. At the doorway I turned and said, "Joanne, I love you." I didn't say it to feel superior or to make her feel more guilt. But I felt that I had to say it to combat my own feelings of animosity and resentment toward her for the pain she had caused me, the pain of not being able to help who I was, the pain of our crumbling friendship.

She said nothing, and I went to the bedroom, feeling as if a part of me had died.

What Joanne had said was serious, so serious that I thought it had crumbled the love and friendship we had built over the years. My mind battled with accepting what she had said and defending my position. No one knew how I felt. No one knew how hard it was to keep asking and asking for help when I wanted to be able just to do whatever I needed to do. I didn't *enjoy* being dependent.

I wanted to go back in and tell Joanne, "It's not fair." I wanted to make her sorry that she had said those things, that she had hurt me. *It's all her fault,* I told myself. *I don't ask her to do much, and I don't assume that she'll do everything for me. And look at all the times I've done stuff for her—letting her use my car whenever she wants, taking her to see her boyfriend, typing her papers and editing them for her, even when I have tons of studying to do. Do I ever say no to her? No. It's not fair!*

Then the next minute, I wanted to cry, because I had been so wrong to a friend without knowing it, because I had lost the love of someone I loved so dearly. The void was wide, and the tears won. "Oh, God," I prayed, "what are You doing? Help me understand."

I began to doubt myself. Was I capable of having a normal friendship? Did all my friends feel the way Joanne did? Was the friendship that I had with her a farce? I felt unanchored and drifting from what I thought was friendship. I couldn't believe that all the laughing, giggling, happy times we'd shared had been counterfeit. This resentment she had against me had been building and had grown so large that it had blocked out the memories of the good times. I had to believe that she had good memories of our friendship—ordering pizzas at midnight, baking cookies for Halloween and Christmas, listening to Johnny Mathis records, writing funny notes to each other and leaving them as surprises on the desks, studying together all night at exam time. *Joanne, please remember,* I cried inside, *please remember.*

Joanne and I avoided each other. Chris and Mary noticed the silence. When they asked me what had happened and I told them, they also bombarded me with similiar feelings of guilt and resentment! They could give me no specific examples, but Mary said that at times my dependency was suffocating. The tears she wept when telling me were sincere.

"I'm sorry Jama, but the Lord told me that if I loved you, I would tell you this. I don't want to hurt you," she said.

"That's okay. I'm not hurt. I understand." I lied. I was hurt and I didn't understand. I held in the tears until she left the room.

Chris made similar remarks, and as I listened to what each said, I got the message: I was too dependent and I irritated everyone.

The isolation I felt was complete. My heart was tattered. *So these are Christian friends?* I thought bitterly. I studied for classes and worked at the store, but I withdrew into the shadows of rejection. I couldn't see beyond my own hurt. I couldn't see that perhaps God was working through this situation, not just to create a certain character in me, but also to work in the lives of Joanne, Mary, and Chris, to cleanse them and create a more Christ-like nature.

Since I thought I was the problem behind all the tension and strife in the apartment, it seemed reasonable that if I moved home we'd all be happier. *My family are the only ones who understand and love me the way I am right now,* I told myself. But I didn't want Mom and Dad to think I was a quitter.

I had told Mom what the girls had said, and she told me that if I wanted to move home, it was all right. For comfort's sake I wanted to, but for pride's sake, I didn't. Then, I adopted the attitude that I lived in the apartment alone. *I won't ask anyone for help and I won't assume that anyone will do anything for me.* In my defensiveness, I took the stand, *If that's the way you want it, I don't need any help. I don't need anyone.* The island of isolation was self-made.

When I had to do the laundry, I did it alone. Instead of suggesting to one of the girls that we do it together, so I wouldn't have to carry everything in and out of the Laundromat by myself, I waited until everyone was out of the apartment. That way they wouldn't see me struggling with the bags of laundry, the box of soap, the hangers. I didn't want them to assume that I wanted any help. And I didn't want them to feel guilty if they didn't feel like helping.

I decided that I could divide up the laundry and put it in at least two plastic trash bags. Then I could put the soap, softener, and hangers in a separate bag. That way I could carry everything to the car more easily. I still had to make three trips, but no one had to help me.

When grocery shopping, I asked the checker to put my items in several sacks. Then I could carry them into the apartment without asking anyone to go out to the car to bring them in for me. I bought cans of pop instead of bottles because I could carry them. I wasn't strong enough yet to carry the weight of pop bottles for a long distance.

Of course, my new independence was based on the wrong attitude: thinking that I didn't need anyone. I was taut inside, pulled one way by the expectations and demands of others, and then the other way by my own desperate attempt to preserve my self-worth. I had yet to find that balance of give-and-take in a relationship, a balance of need that eases tension. In my hurt, rejected state I was reserved and held my roommates at arm's length.

But God was invading my defenses, spanning the breach of my alienation. He was whittling at my wrong attitudes, until I saw the core of loneliness and arrogance in trying to be self-sufficient. I finally saw that *He* is my sufficiency. After the girls released their feelings, I clenched my sufficiency tightly, determined to prove myself. Then I realized that I had to let go of my control and accept His control. I could not receive the full and authentic joy of friendship with a clenched heart.

The tension eased, and I had a clearer vision of the situation as I became more willing to trust the Lord concerning my relationships. My friends' honesty had forced me to reevaluate the way I treated people as a result of my pride. Pride was a tall Jericho wall that needed to tumble down. I knew that I still needed help at certain times, but I had to overcome pride and ask directly for that help, without assuming.

The Lord transformed the bitterness and hurt in my bruised heart into a triumphant shout of victory that declared the miracle of His love. Suddenly, supernaturally, I loved each of the girls with a measure of His holy love that I could not explain. My ego still wanted to punish them for hurting me, but my heart knew forgiveness and gentleness. I had the surprising knowledge that God was able to feed me in the wilderness, that I might be humbled and proven, and that good would come to me in the latter end (Deuteronomy 8:16).

I felt much better about myself, knowing that I could do such things as the laundry, grocery shopping, and cleaning without asking for or assuming I'd get help. I had to do each in an unorthodox manner and it took me longer, but that didn't matter. As long as I allowed God's creativity to operate and accepted the difficulties, He was faithful to give me strength.

My self-confidence and worth were boosted when I thought about graduation and having to make it in the working world. I no longer feared taking a job in another city or the possibility of having to accept more responsibility than I'd ever had before.

Once I relinquished the hurts and rejection and doubts to God and became receptive to His inexhaustible mercy, I broke through the barrier of resentment and could be understanding to Joanne, Mary, and Chris. Whatever motive they might have had or whatever the Lord was working out in their own lives and in their relationships with Him, God had used their honesty about my dependency for my good. We were all learning the importance of honest communication.

Joanne's honesty about her guilt and resentment cleansed our relationship and affected my relationships with Mary and Chris. But it took time for Joanne to work through her feelings. Our friendship had not been a farce. It went through a death and was resurrected into newness. Once she had revealed the corroding resentment, then we were able to deal with it. By talking honestly, we were able to stop the boomerang of self-condemnation caused by guilt feelings. There was pain in revelation, but there was truth. And we were learning and growing because of our pain. God was breaking open new areas of growth and then giving us the strength to dare to move on.

What Joanne, Mary, and Chris resented was not my person—not Jama—but the constant encroachment that my dependency caused on their freedom. Unconsciously, I had been manipulating and controlling others by doing favors that would cause them to say yes to my need for help. By letting everyone use my car, by buying little gifts, by lending money, I was rationalizing that they would be obligated to me, that they would "owe" me. I thought this made me seem less dependent on them. They needed me too, or at least I wanted them to.

But I was learning that bribing others to do things was wrong, and they were learning that actions out of guilt were wrong—both bred an unhealthy friendship. Our new lines of communication were teaching us what it takes to build an honest relationship. Our giving and receiving must be through love and mercy. There must be a balance so that no one feels leaned on too much.

Learning all of this was very painful, but it was well worth it. The pain, the irritation, the discomfort of life in the apartment during those four months together with Joanne, Chris, and Mary resulted in a relationship with each that became something of value. As layers of time, patience, prayer, maturity, and love have covered the pain, all the irritations were like those which cause the creation of a pearl. And ours is a pearl of great price, a pearl of friendship which is stronger and more precious than any of us has ever known. I am truly wealthy; each of them has become a forever friend. God brought us together and covered the hurts with His love.

That fall, Mary moved to Texas because of a job transfer, but neither distance nor time has dissolved our friendship. We both have come to know how much God helped us mature during the time we lived together. We know it takes courage to be honest with friends. I even drove down to Texas by myself the following January to see her, and it was a time that helped stabilize our relationship even more. Throughout it all, Jesus has been the cohesive element.

In November after autumn quarter finals, Joanne moved home to Fort Wayne to do her student teaching. For many months our correspondence was cordial and superficial. Then, during the following January of 1978, she became engaged. She came down to visit and to show me her ring; she also asked me to be the guest book hostess at her wedding. From then on, the Lord seemed to use time to wipe away hurts, and ironically, the separation brought us closer together. We have both obtained a level of maturity that has allowed us to forgive and forget the hurt and resentment.

Some time after she got married, she visited me again, and we had an opportunity to talk about the health of our once fractured friendship.

"You know, Joanne, the older I get, the more I realize how important communication is. Do you realize that we probably wouldn't be sitting here eating pizza and laughing and having a good time, if God hadn't shown us how necessary it is to be honest with the people we care about?"

"I know. We've both grown up a lot. Being in college wasn't always easy. I had a difficult time getting adjusted to being a 'nobody' on such a large campus. At home I felt loved and accepted and special. Because there are six kids in our family, almost everyone knew who I was. I no longer felt special. It was hard for me. Then suddenly I was away from my family and everyone who knew me. And do you know what? When we lived together, I was jealous of you because you got so much of the attention that I wanted, because everyone considered you so special."

"You're kidding! You were jealous of me? It was the other way around. You always had the guys stopping by to see you."

Joanne nodded. "But that's the way I felt. I know looking back I seem like a spoiled kid, but I just needed someone to tell me that I was special, even if I hadn't been in an accident and hadn't been through what you had. What I really needed was for God to tell me that He loved me as much as He loved you, that I was special to Him too."

"You know that you're special to Him now, don't you?" I was marveling that she had grappled with such feelings.

"Oh, yes, I guess I really knew it all along deep down, but I was going through the insecurity and frustration and loneliness of being separated from my family and of trying to grow up. I hadn't really learned to trust in God's sovereignty."

Sharing and talking about the past brought back no pain, only a thankfulness in my heart for the joy of reconciliation. I was glad we had the maturity and courage to wait and work through our hurts. We had not given up on our friendship when it didn't go smoothly. We had learned that our friendship couldn't be based on memories or expectations. It had to be based on the foundation of Christ's love, which had healed our relinquished hearts. In a miraculous way, the pain of our honesty in the apartment became an accolade to herald our growth and our sustaining friendship.

Chris, too, admitted that she had been jealous of me, and that the jealousy had contributed to her resentment and had blocked our friendship. We were all yearning for love and acceptance, for the affirmation that we were special. As we each gave God more and more room in our lives, the affirmation of our self-worth became a bastion of truth.

As Chris matured and yielded more of her life to God, she realized that she had to accept me for who I was just as she knew I had accepted her. Our relationship was growing in joy and peace because of the work we were allowing Christ to do in our emotions and spirits by His mercy and grace. We knew that Jesus had healed us and that we could love one another even with our faults because of Him. His love demanded action. And through love, we stepped beyond our vulnerability and took the initiative to communicate and to provide acceptance and affirmation.

After we all moved from the apartment, our times together were not many, but they were special. As we grew in Him, we grew toward each other. What we had discovered about ourselves and about relationships while in the apartment was immense and life-changing. We all learned in a crucible of pain, frustration, and struggling that any kind of relationship takes honesty and love. Every solid relationship needs an emblem of affirmation and forgiveness; it needs Jesus as the center.

That seemed to be the pattern in the healing of each friendship with Joanne, Mary, and Chris. The closer we walk in knowledge of Him, the closer we walk in knowledge of Love; then the closer we can walk with each other.

17

John

After graduation in November of 1977, I had started working full time at my mom's store, the Happiness Hut. All the resumés I kept sending out applying for various writing positions were coming back with the same answer, "We have nothing now, but we'll keep your name on file." Since my degree was a departmental one in literature and not in English education, I couldn't accept a teaching job. Besides, I wanted to write, but my free-lance poetry sales didn't provide enough money to buy a sack of groceries.

But I was hopeful and confident that God's promises would take care of me. The anxieties about what to do after graduation had dissolved to dust and blown away. For the time being, I was happy to work at the store and on my writing. And life in the apartment was happier since the tension had dissipated and we were communicating our feelings more instead of letting them build up.

Working in the store with Mom and Mac (short for Maxine) was fun, but it seemed to be the last place to meet any eligible men. So it was a pleasant surprise when I met John. In March I started noticing that he came in frequently to browse or buy a card after he had visited The Book Shop, another store on the upper level of our shopping complex. Because I'm curious and friendly by nature, I tried to tell myself I was just being sociable when I asked his name and introduced myself. All the while, however, I was very aware that he was handsome, a lanky six feet two inches, with thick blond hair and deep blue eyes.

Gradually, John started stopping in just to chat, making no pretenses of wanting to buy anything. He stood at the front

counter where I worked the cash register. And when I had cus-
tomers, he wandered to the back of the store where Mom and Mac
worked on silk flower arrangements. They both thought he was
wonderful.

It got to be that every day between four-thirty and five, Mom
would begin glancing out the window. I tried to ignore her, knowing very well the matchmaking tricks she was up to.

"Jama! Here he comes. I just saw his car pull into a parking
place."

I, too, had seen the familiar green car and had quickly combed
my hair.

"Mom, maybe he just needs a card or something."

"And maybe he just wants to ask you out." Both Mom and Mac
wore hopeful grins.

"You guys! Quit grinning like that. He's friendly, that's all.
Lately whenever he's stopped in, he's talked to you more than to
me."

"He's working up his confidence," Mac said. "We've got our
eyes on him and we see how much he likes you. You two book-
worms have a lot in common."

I wasn't sure whether John lacked confidence, or just wanted
to take his time about asking me out. But that spring I had my
own problems with mustering up confidence. My father had
started talking to me about graduate school back in January, but
I hadn't been quite ready then. Finally, in April, Dad persuaded
me to go to the Graduate Office in Ball State's administration
building to sign up for a summer school class to begin my Master
of Arts degree. While I was there, my advisor called the English
department and discovered an opening for a graduate assistant.

As I walked from the building to my car, I marveled at the
decision I had made. I was not only a graduate student, but also
had an assistantship for the 1978–79 school year. As an assistant,
I would have to teach a freshman composition course, which
would pay for my tuition while I was taking my own courses.
Since I had never taught before and had no student teaching or
educational courses, I would be stepping on new ground. But a

voice inside me said, *"Yes, I can do this."* I knew that I must really be growing up. New experiences held less fear.

But accepting an assistantship was not the only new ground I would be stepping on. There was John and a possible new relationship with a man. During my last few years in college, God had softened my anxiousness about dating. I had abandoned the insecurity that had taunted me with feelings of being undesirable. I knew that God knew my heart, and I surrendered to Him my desire to be married one day, and once I had done that, I knew I couldn't fret. Again, I had to wait in patience.

Whether he did need time to gather confidence, or whether he had another reason, it wasn't until late June that John finally asked me out.

As usual on first dates, we talked and talked, filling in background information that we hadn't mentioned in earlier brief conversations. I knew that most people were curious about what had happened to me, so I brought up the subject of my accident, feeling that John would be too polite to ask. I gave God the glory for His power to heal and for what He had done for me. John didn't ask too many questions but listened attentively.

During the evening, John's consideration and gentleness marked his maturity. At twenty-eight, he was the oldest guy who'd ever asked me out; the six-year age difference only seemed to give us more to talk about. His quick wit and gallant courtesy made me feel comfortable. I didn't feel self-conscious because he looked into my eyes while we walked and not at the slowness or awkwardness of my walking.

As we were together more and more throughout the summer—picnicking, going to movies, playing miniature golf, eating out—it was almost as if there was nothing physically different about me. John never said anything like, "Oh, you can't do that." He was patient concerning my slow walking, and he knew that he had to allow a little more time when we went somewhere. He gave me attention as no other guy had, sending me surprise cards, bringing over a Cookie Monster cake to celebrate our first month of dating. His kindness and generosity didn't end with me, but extended to my roommates. To give us a break from studying, John made us all rubber band guns and brought us balsa wood glider planes. Acting like little kids with the guns and gliders was great fun and just the relaxation we needed.

Because I did live with three girls, John and I were rarely alone in the apartment. John lived on the first floor of a house, and we often went there to fix dinner or to watch a movie on TV. But the more we saw of one another, the more we both felt the physical pressures of a caring relationship between a man and woman. To alleviate this pressure, most evenings after we had gone to eat or to a movie, I suggested that we go back to my apartment where I knew we probably wouldn't be alone.

When school started in the autumn, I had a new pressure— teaching. I had gained more confidence about talking in front of groups since I had gone with Mom on several of her speaking engagements and had shared my testimony. But I felt inadequate and frightened in the role of instructor. I knew I could do it, but it was getting the materials to do it with. I had no files of grammar drills or quizzes or lecture notes on expository modes of writing. I had been exempt from the first composition course when I was in college because of my verbal SAT score, so I didn't even have that experience to fall back on.

A combination of pressures and responsibilities to teach well and to study for high grades all seemed to push me away from John. I knew I couldn't give him the attention he needed and deserved. All my effort was concentrated on school, and I felt guilty when I was with John because I knew I had so much work to do—preparing class lectures, grading student themes, reading assigned books, writing essays.

But deep inside, I knew and didn't want to admit that I was using my new responsibilities as an excuse to give me time to think. My relationship with John had developed so fast that at first all I did was enjoy it rather than analyze it. Now, I needed time to think and clear my head, to pray and understand my heart. Suddenly, the fact that John wasn't a professing Christian, even with his abundance of goodness, made a blatant difference.

I had asked him about his faith and he had told me that he

believed in God and had experienced His presence, but he wasn't sure what he believed about Jesus.

"If you don't believe in Jesus as the Christ and as your Savior, then you're not a Christian," I had said.

"No, I guess not."

My heart had saddened and ached for his soul. We had long talks on our religious differences, and I was confused about where our relationship should go, since I knew I was not to be "unequally yoked."

I had joked with him, "I'll see you in November when this quarter is over." But the joke turned into reality when he stopped coming by the apartment and calling. Although I was busy with school, I couldn't help but think about John, wondering if he would reenter my life in November, or if he thought we had too many differences to reconcile.

Autumn quarter came and went, and I heard no word from John. The winter quarter began, and my life became less hectic as far as school was concerned. I had switched my winter teaching assignment (assistants teach only two of the three quarters) to the spring so I would have more time to work on my creative thesis project. I was also taking only one class. The rest and relaxation were welcomed, but suddenly I had more time to think about John. A sorrow and hurt rolled into my heart, and I thought that he probably never wanted to see me again because of my aloof attitude the last few times that we had been together. I asked God to forgive me and debated whether to call John and ask him to forgive me too.

On the last day of November, I was just putting on my coat to go to my night class when I heard a faint knock on the front door. No one was home but me, so from the kitchen I shouted, "Come on in. The door's open."

I stood in the doorway with one arm in my coat sleeve, waiting to see who it was. I almost grabbed the chair I was standing by to steady myself as I saw John's blond head peer around the door.

"Hi," his voice was soft. "You did say come in, didn't you?"

"Well, hi. Gosh, I didn't expect . . . yes, come on in. How are you?" My words fumbled over one another.

While he was walking across the living room, I put my other arm into its coat sleeve. He stood in front of me, and I couldn't believe he was there. He seemed more handsome than ever.

"I'm fine. How are you? I see you made it through the quarter."

"Yes, I'm glad it's over. I've got a night class tonight, but I'm not teaching this quarter," I said.

"I told you I'd see you in November. Today's the day."

We were silent, neither one knowing quite what to say next. I looked up and our eyes met.

"John, it's so good to see you."

The next thing I knew his arms had encircled me and he was hugging me tightly. "Oh, Jama, Jama," he whispered. "I've missed you. It's so good to hold you again."

The hug was long and warm, a hug to reconcile all the misunderstandings and the separation. And then, still leaning his tall frame over me, he kissed me. I wanted to go into the living room, sit on the couch, and talk quietly with him for hours. I wanted to make up for all the time that we had been apart. But my night class started in fifteen minutes.

"May I see you tomorrow?" John asked after he had walked me to my car. "Would you like to go out to eat?"

"Of course you may, and yes I'd love to eat with you. I'll be here all day."

I smiled and giggled and thanked God as I drove to class. Trying to concentrate on the lecture was almost impossible!

The December Christmas season became very special as John and I saw more of each other. We talked about what had happened in our relationship and decided that we would take things more slowly, that we would just enjoy each other for the time being. We knew that we still had too many differences to make any immediate decisions about where our relationship was going.

I was still unsure of my feelings. John had asked me what I wanted out of our relationship, and I evaded the question by saying, "I want us both to be happy." But my heart knew what I wanted. I wanted John in my future, but I wanted a Christian John. One night after John brought me back to the apartment, I talked to God about it. From the kitchen window, I stared at the moon as it shone with bright radiance, a circle of light haloed its fullness. The circle stretched out far into the black sky, spanning the heavens.

"Lord, You alone know what's ahead for me. And You know how much I'm beginning to care about John, but I'm scared because I don't want to care *too* much since he's not a Christian. I know that You love him, and what I want for him above all else is that he would know Christ. If nothing serious ever happens in our relationship, if You brought us together for the singular purpose of his salvation, that's still what I want. I don't know if John knows that.

"Lord, I know You want the very best for John and I claim his salvation for You. Be with me. Help me to be patient. I have a peace that it's Your will for us to be seeing each other again. But help me not to worry. You are God. I love You. Amen."

We ushered in 1979 together with a tender kiss at midnight. The moments with John were becoming more precious and I thought about him throughout the day, anticipating the evening when I would get to see him. I thought about his gentleness and his caring, about his warm hugs, about the look in his eyes when he bent down to kiss me. He was so good, so gracious that he *seemed* like a Christian. *But seeming and confessing are not synonymous,* I told myself. My emotions were jumbled and I couldn't explain my feelings about John. Being with him was beginning to feel so right, and I was flustered as a result.

But the more we were together, the more I knew I loved John in spite of our differences. Because we both knew that our relationship had developed into something deeper than merely dating to be dating, we knew that we couldn't keep sidestepping our obvious conflict. We had to confront it more directly. Most of the time I brought up the subject that resulted in our serious talks when I asked him to go to church with me.

"You know, John, the barrier between us is bothering me more and more," I said as he held me in his arms on the couch. "We share so many good times together and we can talk about most anything. But we can't talk about the area of my life that means the most to me. The Lord has done so much in my life that I just can't stifle the desire to talk about Him and to share Him. And now that you're such a part of my life, I want so desperately for us to be able to share in His love and goodness together. Talking with my girl friends is great, but I would feel such a closer unity with you if *we* could share the excitement of the Bible and walking with God."

"Jama," he began as he stroked my cheek, "I know your Christian beliefs are strong and a major part of your life, but the difference you're talking about doesn't matter that much to me. I can accept our differences, even though I know how you feel. But I just can't include your beliefs in my own life right now. I guess it goes back to one of the reasons I left the church when I was in college, because of all the hypocrisy I saw there. I believe in God, I've told you that. But that's all for right now."

We were silent for a while, holding each other, knowing our love even amidst the barrier. The spirit within me was all one petition that John might open the door to Jesus, for only by knowing Jesus could he truly know God.

"Jama, I want a future with you. But I know we've got some things to work out."

"The difference matters a lot, John, maybe more than you know. It would be much easier if I could accept it as you do, but I can't. You're on one side and I'm on the other. I can't erase what I know about the Bible's attitude toward marriage and how important a marriage is in the eyes of God. It is in His design, but the man and woman must be like-minded for the relationship to have complete unity. I know that the man I marry must share the same foundation. God says that the two will become one, and I want to be one with my husband in every sense: mental, emotional, physical, and especially spiritual. It's that spiritual bond that connects a couple with the power of God and that can help pull them through any problems in any of the other areas.

"As you can see, I've been doing a lot of thinking about this. I do love you, John. But Jesus loves you so much more, more than I ever could. And He wants you to be His."

He said nothing but hugged me tightly. I prayed for wisdom and for John to receive the legacy of His Love.

In March John was transferred from the Muncie office of the Indiana Employment Security Division to the office in Peru, two hours away. Since his parents live in Gas City, an hour from Peru, John decided to live with them and keep his apartment in Muncie, hoping to arrange a transfer back. This transfer meant that we would be together only on weekends.

Because our time together was suddenly shortened, we spent less of it talking about our "spiritual difference" and more filling each other in on what had happened during the week. It was easy for both of us to feel depressed when we concentrated too much energy on our conflict.

Spring watered the growth of our relationship, and I felt perfumed with love. But I also felt the pressure of the approaching deadline for my Master's thesis creative project. I had been enjoying my weekends with John so much that I had no impelling motivation to seclude myself and write. School was out now, and the realization that I had six weeks to finish my project shocked me into action. I decided to accept the offer of some friends in Wisconsin to drive up there to visit and write. They offered me their study, their typewriter, and the uninterrupted quiet I needed.

During the three weeks I was at the Tregoning's, my work was productive, and I delighted in the friendship of Joe and Jeanne and their little boy Joshua. But I also missed John terribly. We wrote long letters and sent cards to one another, yet a deep loneliness filled me. My prayers that God was continually working in his heart climaxed in a crescendo of hope: I did not want to go through life without him. Many others were also praying for John, standing in faith with me that he would surrender the control of his life to Christ.

I knew John's salvation was only a matter of time. *Soon, soon, Lord,* I prayed, feeling my love for John swell to dwarf the many differences I had thought were so separating. His absence made me cherish his uniqueness. The only major gap between us now would be bridged when he made a commitment to Christ.

After I completed my thesis project, summer beckoned with fun and activities, especially several weddings involving my friends and family. John attended all of them with me, but not without some reluctance. Easy and relaxed around me or Mom or Mac, he found it hard to fit in at social gatherings where he was a little older than most of my crowd and a complete stranger.

In August I received my Master of Arts degree and was hired by the Ball State English Department to teach two composition courses during each quarter. I was feeling more comfortable in the teaching role, more competent that the students were learning about grammar and effective writing. God had directed me into an area that I was finding surprisingly rewarding.

And I had to keep believing that God was directing me in my relationship with John. We were both working hard at trying to please each other, and our love was growing because of the effort. But still there was that gulf between us, that expanse between our spirits. Our love for each other could not close that gap, only Jesus could.

My love urged me to talk more boldly to John about Jesus. He listened with patience and gentleness as I almost sermonized about Jesus and His goodness and what He had done for me and what He could do for him. But no amount of my talking and sharing seemed to make a difference; John was not ready to make a decision. The more I talked, the more stubborn he seemed to get. It was not me he was resisting as much as the knowledge that asking Jesus into his heart meant surrendering the complete control of his life. That concept was immense and frightening.

Although we both laughed and joked about the "big M" of marriage, we knew the underlying seriousness. John knew that he dare not make an official proposal. He knew I could not say yes until I was sure that our marriage foundation would be in Christ, and he could not yet give me that assurance. The limbo period of waiting, our future together in the balance, stretched my heart and hope. At times, I would rest in the assurance that God answers prayers. And then, when I would see John's disinterest and stiffness while in church or when I shared, I would be bombarded with disappointment.

My mom knew the struggling and the frustration that waiting could bring. She knew that I loved John, and I often reached out to her for comfort and encouragement. She and Dad were my staff of faithful support, steadfast in the desire for my happiness. They were acolytes to brighten my flame which was dimmed too often by frustration.

"Mom," I was almost in tears when I called her on the phone. "Mom, he didn't want to go to church this morning. He wanted to do his laundry. I keep thinking that he's edging toward the Lord because we're starting to be more open and having more talks about the Lord, and then he says he doesn't want to go to church. I just don't know what to do. I've prayed, claimed, fasted, cried, pouted. I feel him pressuring me about marriage, but he knows I can't say yes. Oh Mom, I'm so frustrated. Why do I always have to *wait* so long for everything?"

She listened without interrupting while I rambled. "I don't know, honey," she chuckled. "You do seem to get your patience exercised, huh? But I've been praying about this too. I know that waiting for someone to open up to Christ is especially hard when it's someone you love. But what I think you should try is blessing him. When he says he doesn't want to go to church, bless him. When he is stubborn, bless him. Just keep blessing him. Maybe you'll bless him right into the Kingdom! Let the Lord do the work, Jama. Don't try to do it for Him."

I listened to Mom's wisdom and began blessing more than pestering. Just as I had learned to wait and be patient for the consistently dependable and perfectly punctual control of God concerning my healing, so I had to apply that guiding truth to John. Once again I had to utterly trust His sovereignty. I became less consumed with being the one to personally usher John into the Kingdom, and decided to let God work on his heart without my steady interference.

The times together with John were not all serious talks. The autumn was full of activities other than discussing our relationship. John had been transferred back to the Muncie office so we had more time to enjoy the love we did share even with the gap between us. We went to Ball State's football games and down to Louisville to visit my friends Cheri and Tony. I went with him to his family's birthday celebrations, and he went with me to my grandparents' for Thanksgiving.

That autumn I also moved home with my family. Although the independence of living in an apartment was gratifying, I was frustrated because I never seemed to have enough money. Because I didn't want to teach full-time, but wanted to have time to work on my poetry and writing, my salary was not enough to pay the bills. Mom and Dad both encouraged the move, and I looked forward to having the extra money to buy the contact lenses I wanted and to take a writing course at Earlham College.

Being home with Mom, Dad, Doug, and Julee was wonderful and relaxing. And by now, John was feeling right at home with them. But the time that John and I had always spent alone was suddenly filled with people. We had fewer serious discussions and more light, joking dialogues with the family. In a way, I was relieved that we had less time alone because of the strong physical pull that our love created. I knew my moral and Biblical boundaries, and John's love for me respected those limitations, yet the frustration was still there for both of us.

To compensate for our lack of time alone and the decrease in quiet talks together, I suggested that we both keep journals of our feelings and thoughts to share with one another. John didn't seem too enthusiastic, but he was willing to work at deepening our relationship.

And the deepening came. Because of our effort, because of our love, because of the Lord. By sharing in our journals, we were able to express on paper what we were sometimes not able to talk about. John peeled away the membranes that covered the feelings he had long kept inside, and I realized again what a sensitive, caring man he was. His intelligence was etched in his words, and the strength of his love for me filled the pages. I saw that his love was not controlled by his sexual passions, but that his love controlled his sexual desire because he knew that I could only give that kind of physical commitment through marriage.

Love for God, however, was something John grappled with in honest sincerity. Believing that God exists wasn't the problem; nor did basic Christian doctrines give him a lot of trouble. The issue was the Lordship of Christ. John knew Jesus was supposed to be more than a Savior, but he could not take the step that would include making Him Lord.

Nonetheless, God was doing a tender work in our relationship, taking that wide difference that separated us and using it to mold our love into a love that was strong and patient, good for our latter end. The waiting became longer than I expected, but I had to remember that faith comes before sight, that faith honors God. I had to expect that an end would come to my faithful waiting.

I prayed that 1980 would be John's year of decision, but the winter turned to spring and no declared decision came. John was grappling with relinquishment, knowing the weight of a commitment to Christ. And he knew that I was riveted to my beliefs and there could be no compromise.

One night in late spring, I reminded God one more time where I stood. "I love John, Lord, and I will not let go of him. I'm going to be like Jacob and I won't let go. I'll wait. It's hard, but I'll wait. And I know the unity You will ultimately bring to us will be worth everything. For our love is surely being tempered in a fire."

I hung on tenaciously to my love for John, and yet I was more aware that God was the one hanging on to me, gracing me with a faith that was unassailable by the situation. I finally surrendered John completely to God and relaxed. I knew that God in His crowning creativity would act. I knew I was going to marry John, because I could never love a man the way I loved John.

Late in May we were at John's apartment, sitting together on the couch. I decided to try to relieve some of the tension and so I said, "I will wait forever for you to come to Christ if that's what it takes. I don't understand why you don't want all the love and joy and security that He offers right now, but I'll wait until you decide that risking your future by putting it into His hands is really no risk at all. And I've decided that I won't bring up this subject again until you tell me that you've made a decision. As much as I love to talk about the Lord, I won't. Not until you want to."

John sat for what seemed a long time. Then he said, "Thanks, Jama, that's what I need. I'm stubborn, I guess. I just dig in my heels when I feel pressured."

A week or two later, in early June, we were together again and somehow the conversation got on families and raising children. John surprised me by saying that our home would be a Christian home if we got married.

"Does that mean that you've made a decision that you want to tell me about?" I asked, my heart on tiptoe.

"Don't pressure me, okay? But I want to marry you."

"Is this a proposal?"

"Not yet, because I know what you'll say."

I prayed, *Lord, help me not to pressure him.* But my heart was sensing a change. John sang the hymns in church with more conviction, and we analyzed the sermons on the way home.

All during June we seemed to talk more and more about what marriage together would be like. We were cheerful and positive, both certain of its inevitability. I teased him that Mom and I needed at least two or three months to plan a wedding.

"Do you know that Mom's picked out August 30 as the day we should get married? She's even picked out the colors I should have, can you believe it?"

"Of your mother? Yes, I can believe it."

"Well, if you want to get married this summer before I start teaching again, then you'd better hurry up and make a decision. Not that I want to pressure you or anything," I teased. "But do you *really* want to wait until the quarter break in November to get married?"

John smiled, but didn't say anything. Was he digging in his heels again, or was there a different look in his eye? I couldn't tell. My feelings were a mass of confusion. I was eager to get married; I was just as eager that he know Christ. The one couldn't happen without the other. I knew that and so did John. And we both knew he would have to mean it. I would just have to keep on waiting.

A few days later John and I were riding in his car. It was Wednesday, June 25, and we were going out to dinner. While I chattered on as usual, John was silent. Finally it occurred to me that he had something he wanted to say—if only I would give him a chance.

"I wanted to tell you this on our two-year anniversary of knowing one another," he began. "I thought it was tonight, but just before we left your mother said that you told her it wasn't until this Saturday—on the twenty-eighth."

My stomach was an instant mass of butterflies. "Go ahead, tell me now. We'll pretend it's today. I can't believe you're so sentimental, and I can't believe that you're actually going to tell me what I think you are while we're driving in your *car!*"

"Well, you know it's hard for me to put some things into words. . . ."

Three different versions of what I hoped John would say leaped into my mouth, but somehow I left them there, waiting for him to say it, his way.

"I've been wrestling with becoming a real Christian, not the halfway kind. It's been hard to sort out my feelings for you and my feelings about that. I didn't want to become a Christian just to marry you. But I really do want to marry you. It's hard to explain, but I have decided that I do want Jesus to be my Lord. I've accepted Him in my life, and if you want to start in on the wedding plans you can." His words ran together in one burst of relief and joy.

My heart shouted, *Praise God!* for the final answer to the millions of prayers I must have prayed. Billows of love swept over me with a fullness of hope and beauty and eternity, with a glory that completes a longing. "Oh John, I love you," I said. "You are a fulfillment of God's promise to me, the answer to my heart's desire. Our love is His love."

John reached his hand across the seat and clasped mine tightly. "I love you, Jama."

The summer night was a precious green harmony.

Epilogue

Dad's hand is gently quivering as it covers my hand which is cradled in the bend of his elbow. "Don't look down as you walk, Jama," he whispers. "I know. I keep wanting to, too, but look straight ahead."

I raise my head and we walk slowly side by side. I feel the eyes of many as they watch us. My smile broadens. The organ music swells. As we pass friends and relatives, many are crying. It is August 30, 1980—my wedding day.

The aisle seems endless. My bouquet is in my left hand, and I tightly grip Dad's arm with my right. I want no crutch in my wedding ceremony! Passing Joanne, her husband Rick, and their four-month-old baby Jared, I wink at her; her eyes are shining.

Dad and I slowly proceed as the wedding march is repeated. Mom stands in the first pew, and the lump in my throat tightens. Her face is all love and our smile is as one.

John stands with our minister Martin Brown in front of the altar. Our eyes meet as I approach. Our love transcends our nervousness. We smile. I have never seen him look so handsome. His six feet two inches is impressive in the silver gray tuxedo, and all else seems superfluous as Dad and I take the last few steps to meet him. Praise to God ascends from within. I feel encompassed and blazing with love. *Oh, John, how I love you!* I can't stop smiling!

Julee, my maid of honor, stands on my left. She is incredibly beautiful and mature. Now, at nineteen, she is closer and more dear to me than ever, a true friend. God could give me no better sister.

The music quiets as Dad stands between John and me. Martin asks us to pray. I look up at John, and we close our eyes.

"Father, we thank you today because it is by the power of Your Spirit that John and Jama have come together to be united in marriage. We praise You. We thank You because it is by Your love and Your grace that this has all been possible. And as they join together today, we pray that You would join them by a special miracle of Your love and Your grace, that all who are present here would know that Jesus Christ is alive because He lives in their lives and has brought them to this moment in joy and love. We praise You and we thank You for these things in Jesus' name. Amen."

Martin reads from the Book of Ephesians, chapter five, and I know what a tremendous responsibility we are entering into. But I also know that God has made us ready; He is the One uniting us.

When Martin says, "Who gives this woman to be married to this man," I turn and meet Dad's eyes; overwhelming love and gratitude for this man surge through me. In this moment I think how pleased God must be with the man He created to be my father.

Dad focuses on me; our eyes speak our hearts. "Her mother and I." Our lips meet in a kiss, and he places my hand in John's. I fight back the tears, pursing my lips and smiling. John looks down at me and knows.

Through the songs, through the affirmation of our vows, I see only John and the miracle of our love which God has created. We stand facing each other, our hands clasped. His hands are slightly shaking and cold. In a paradox of emotions, we are nervous and yet wrapped in a wonderful peace. Quietly, John speaks the vows from his heart.

"Here, among family and friends, I, John, vow to you, Jama, at the beginning of our marriage, that I will love you with all my heart and honor you and work together with you throughout the

rest of our lives, increasing our faith in God and our union together. I am your husband. I love you."

My eyes are moist. I smile and speak, "Today, among our
friends and our family, I vow and pledge to be the best wife to you
that I can, to love you in times of tears and laughter, through
struggles and successes, to be one with you as I never have with
anyone before. I want to help you grow, as you have helped me
grow, that our marriage may be fresh and exciting. You were
designed by God to be the king and priest of our family, and as
such, I will submit and obey you as my head. Christ has brought
our love together, and in Him will our love and our marriage be
strengthened and sustained. I am your helpmate; I am your wife.
I love you."

Our ceremony of love and joy continues. We exchange rings and
Martin pronounces that John and I are husband and wife. My
mind repeats those two words, knowing that today they apply to
John and me. Inside is a continuous song of praise to my God who
has blessed me so abundantly with this man.

As the first act of our married life, John and I partake of
communion, then we listen as Cheri, one of my bridesmaids and
a past roommate, joins with her husband, Tony, to sing Amy
Grant's song, "There Will Never Be Another." I feel a purer
measure of God's love than I have ever felt before—for Him, for
John, for my friend Cheri. I hear the beauty of Cheri's voice as
a clear beauty from Jesus.

The song ends. Martin says, "You may kiss the bride." I am
taken by surprise at the strong passionate kiss John gives me as
he leans over and wraps his arms around me. It is quite unlike the
peck he gave me during rehearsal. I shake my head and want to
shout "WOW!" Ripples of tickled laughter come from the audience.

Surprise confuses me. Martin laughs and whispers, "Take your
bouquet." Julee hands it to me, and I fumble to hold it properly
in front of my gown. John and I turn and face the audience; my
eyes widen at the large number of people.

I hear Martin's voice behind us. I see Mom and Dad in the front pew. *Please don't cry,* I tell myself. John holds my hand as it rests in the bend of his elbow. We look at each other—all smiles.

"Ladies and gentlemen, it gives me great pleasure to present to you Mr. and Mrs. John E. Bigger."

Then the audience begins applauding with loud claps of happiness. The organ plays and we walk down the aisle together. I am John's wife. I am now Jama Sue Kehoe Bigger. And I am blessed.